MW01135860

The Energy of Emotions

The 10 Emotional Environments and How They
Shape the World Around Us

By
Emily Maroutian

© 2015 © 2017 by Emily Maroutian

All rights reserved. No part of this book may be reproduced, stored in a retrieval system or transmitted in any form or by any means without prior written permission of Emily Maroutian, except in the case of brief quotations embodied in articles or reviews.

ISBN-13: 978-1500203917

Second Printing - Revised

Printed and bound in the United States of America by Createspace, a division of Amazon.com

DISCLAIMER: This book is philosophical in nature, and it contains theories and ideas about the energy of emotions. It is not meant to be a psychological guide or diagnosis for any mental illness. Also, it is not meant to replace therapy or medication. It is a philosophical book intended to inspire discussion and exploration rather than to cure or treat diseases of any kind.

empowered by

Maroutian Entertainment
Los Angeles, California
www.maroutian.com

The Energy of Emotions

The 10 Emotional Environments and How They Shape the World Around Us

By
Emily Maroutian

Books by Emily Maroutian:

A Second Opinion:
Theories and Observations on Life and Human Behavior

The Process of "I":
An Exploration into the Intertwined Relationship between
Identity and Environment

The Energy of Emotions:
The 10 Emotional Environments and How They Shape the
World Around Us

Thirty:
A Collection of Personal Quotes, Advice, and Lessons

The Empowered Self:
Over 100 Activities and Steps For Creating An Empowered
Mind

The Book of Relief:
Passages and Exercises to Relieve Negative Emotion and
Create More Ease in The Body

Acknowledgements:

I would like to acknowledge all of the people who have supported my spiritual journey. Our conversations and interactions, whether they were originally perceived as positive or negative, have supported my overall growth. Thank you for your contributions.

Thank you to my family, friends, co-workers, mentors, and partners. I am deeply honored to know you.

A special thank-you to my editor, LaGina Phillips.

Table of Contents:

This book is dedicated to you.
May you find ease and upliftment within these pages.

Introduction:

Emotions are the main driving force in our lives. They control the atmosphere of our relationships, how we talk to people on a daily basis, our working environments, body wellness, how we eat, have sex, the way we relate to others, and whether we have a good day or a bad one.

Feelings are important to our general wellness, as well as our satisfaction with our everyday lives. Our moods change how we feel about everything around us. We have different views of others and ourselves when we are in a good mood verses when we are in a bad one.

We value emotions so much that everything we ever want to possess in life is simply because we want to change our emotions in the moment.

We want to buy a house so we can feel a sense of security or a sense of importance, we want to own an expensive car so we can feel accomplished or cool, we want a relationship so we can feel loved or safe. We don't really want that specific house, car, or relationship; we want the feelings of security, importance, accomplishment, coolness, love, and safety. It's the emotion that feels good, not the item. The item is just our trigger for the emotion. The same item might trigger a different emotion in someone else.

When we look at people and desire their beauty or body, we really just want to feel the way we think they feel in their beauty or body. We want the worthiness, the confidence, the reason to like ourselves, the permission to be more open and expressive. We don't really want their body; we want the emotions we believe are associated with the body.

The Energy of Emotions

We go on vacations for the relaxation or for the exciting feeling of adventure. We buy expensive clothes because it gives us a feeling of importance. We go from relationship to relationship for the feeling of passion and love. We go to expensive schools because it gives us a sense of security for our future. We help others because it makes us feel better about ourselves.

Everything we do is for the emotion we feel or think we will feel as we do it. We have simply attached the feeling to the item or activity and can't see them as two separate things in our minds. We think the only way to receive the feeling is through possessing the item, which is not true.

This doesn't mean we shouldn't want those houses, cars, vacations, or relationships. It just means we can't limit the feelings exclusively to those things, or else we will create pain and suffering when we don't or can't have them.

We prolong unnecessary suffering within us until we possess the thing we want—but what we really want is the feeling behind the item, which won't come because we think it's exclusive to the item we don't have. Instead of finding another route to the feeling, which is always available to us, we choose to fight or suffer until we get the specific thing we want. We delay and deny our happiness because we can't separate our emotions from items, circumstances, and people.

There is more than one way to feel love or security or accomplishment. Moreover, it does not matter whether it's the love we feel for our dogs or for our spouses; the energy of love is the energy of love. It is just as powerful, regardless of what the object of attention is that is eliciting the response within us.

In other words, the energy is not any less powerful if we feel accomplished by cleaning our house or doing our laundry than if we're graduating college or getting a promotion. The distinctions of "big" and "small" are only important in our personal or societal judgments. To energy, emotion is emotion.

Energy doesn't judge the reasons why we feel what we feel. Energy multiplies and feeds more of the same, regardless of what it is or why it is. So feeling accomplished for "little" tasks sets us up to receive opportunities to accomplish "bigger" tasks, which is simply a multiplication of the energy. Feeling love for our dog sets us up to receive opportunities to love a potential spouse. Energy multiplies and feeds itself, so starting "small" only guarantees opportunities for the "big." That's how momentum builds.

Every emotion exists within us and can be summoned at any time. The more we practice them in our everyday experiences, the more we multiply them in our lives. As they multiply, they become bigger and bigger each time. If we don't become discouraged or turn our attention to the desire of what we think we lack, we can multiply the energy quickly.

It is our attention to our feelings that changes them. We often tell ourselves we "shouldn't" feel a certain way. We shame ourselves out of great experiences because we judge ourselves.

We are raised to believe that our emotions are under the control of outside circumstances. We learn to fight people and control situations just so we can experience better-feeling emotions. This makes our emotions dependent on other people's behavior.

We want others to change so we'll feel good about them. However, they desire the same for us. This leaves us in a constant state of conflict or stalemate. We want others to do the work on themselves so we can feel better, but we're less willing to do our own work. That's going about it the hard way.

We fail to recognize that we are the only people who ever had any real control over our emotions. Other people and things can be automatic triggers for certain emotions, but we can change or uninstall triggers. We can become more conscious, we can heal, and we can grow. All of those things are within our control.

We value our emotions more than we value anything else—even other people. In fact, one of the only things we value in others is how they make us feel. Do they make us feel safe or unsafe, loved or ignored, valued or worthless?

There are some feelings we value above others, and we are willing to trade one for another. We accept jobs we don't like because the feeling of security is more valuable to us than our comfort. We may hate smoking, but we do it because the feeling of comfort in smoking is more valuable than the fear of bad health. We buy things we can't afford because the feeling of accomplishment from shopping is more valuable than the pain of debt. We stay in bad relationships because the comfort we feel from being with someone is more valuable than the loneliness and sadness we feel in them.

We are willing to destroy our lives because of our feelings. We are willing to hurt others so that we can feel good. We are even willing to destroy the planet to make ourselves feel wealthier or more powerful.

Emotions rule our existence. An emotion is not simply a mental or energetic occurrence. It is physical, as well.

You can feel anger in your muscles as they tighten. You can feel anxiety in your stomach as a knot. You can feel joy in your heart as it expands. Emotions can make us sick or help us heal.

Our emotions are not merely reactions to the outside world. They are the creative force of our lives. They are energy and come with a powerful ability to shape our bodies, environments, lives, and world.

Emotions are powerful movers of energy because emotions are personal facts. "I am hurt!" is a true statement. We don't generally see emotions as facts because facts tend to be viewed as logical and emotions tend to be viewed as illogical. But even when someone is being rational, they're really just being calm, which is an emotion. The emotional environment inspires the rational thinking. It is a product of the calm emotion. We are always acting through emotion, even when we don't realize it.

We don't give enough attention to calmness because it's not an obvious emotion like rage or joy. When we feel calm, we think that's just us being normal. We fail to realize that we are always feeling something, even when we're feeling numb.

There is nothing illogical about the declaration of emotions because we are feeling 24 hours a day, 7 days a week. We rarely ever say we feel hurt or we feel upset. We declare it as a fact. "I am angry!" We replace the word "feel" with "am" because we have been taught that feelings remove the validity of a statement and we don't want our emotions to feel invalid. It feels more powerful and factual when we declare, "I am angry!" It feels less powerful when we say, "I feel angry!"

Everything we do is for the feeling, so if the feeling is invalid, then there is no purpose in the things we do. This is why we declare emotions as facts. This is also why it's important to validate your own emotions as you move through them. Denying them only keeps them in place for longer periods of time.

Emotions are not invalid. They feel real, and they feel factual, and that is what moves the energy through them. You can't debate someone else's emotions and try to convince them they are not angry when they are. Try it. The next time someone is really angry, say to them, "You're not really angry." See what happens. In almost all cases, it will make them angrier because you are invalidating their feelings.

Using logic or facts and figures doesn't move the energy of an emotion into a better place; only another emotion can do that. One emotion has to ease into another emotion. We can't jump from depression to joy in the same way we can't jump from the first floor to the tenth floor. Depression has to naturally move into a nearby emotion.

We have to ease ourselves through emotions by letting them make their natural climb and not making ourselves wrong for feeling rage or shame. It's when we judge our process that we cycle back and forth between two environments.

As we go through life, we create momentum with certain emotions. For instance, it might become easier to get depressed than to feel joy. Or any little thing can make us angry, and yet we feel like we have to work toward hope. Perhaps we were raised within these environments and we have practiced them all of our lives. Perhaps we don't know any better because momentum has made it easy to feel them.

Momentum is when something builds up speed so much that it requires little effort or action to maintain it. Some people build up momentum on success, joy, and love. It comes so easily to them that others label it as luck or coincidence. Regardless of what they do, everything always seems to work out for them. They've practiced a momentum of ease in these subjects, and so they rarely ever dip down to worry or discouragement when they think about it.

There are others who build momentum in depression or anger so that it takes very little to go to these emotional places. It all depends on which emotion you have been practicing and for how long. Either way, if we don't allow the emotion to naturally move up, we will stay in cycles and begin to create from that environment.

We often leave a subject in an emotional environment and so every time we return to it, it feels the same way. There is no progress in that subject because there is no emotional progress.

We've seen this in the people around us. We know which subjects make them angry, which subjects make them sad. We know just what to say to push other people's buttons. We know that money makes this person anxious, and we know that love makes that person depressed. We know it so well because it's been the same for years, even decades.

We often leave subjects, events, people, and experiences in certain emotional environments thinking that's where they belong. We might think we're supposed to be anxious over money. We're supposed to not trust our spouses. We might think since something was traumatic, we can't feel joy afterward. There is no subject or event that can't be moved into alignment.

Any awful, horrible, upsetting event or circumstance anyone has ever experienced can be moved through the emotional environments into joy, freedom, love, or empowerment. Yes, all of them, even the mass tragedies that seem unthinkable. Everything can be moved into alignment. Some may take years or decades, but it's possible.

The emotional environment determines the possibilities, opportunities, and avenues of the problem or situation. If we keep things in the lower environments, we won't be able to see the opportunities that can move them into alignment or joy. From those environments, it just doesn't seem possible, so we don't do anything about it.

In joy, we see the same thing very differently from when we looked at it in depression. A problem might "feel" like it has no easy answers in anxiety, but in hope it may be so easy we don't even have to think about it. Everything feels different in each environment.

Forgiveness might not seem possible from rage, but it's inevitable in peace. In fact, it's required in peace. Perhaps we can't see the pathways to it just yet, but it's there.

Maybe some part of us is afraid to forgive because we think forgiveness will make us vulnerable again. We think it'll make us put our guards down and open ourselves up for more betrayal. We'll become blind enough to take them back or place ourselves in harmful situations again.

Forgiveness is a kind of detachment. It simply means cutting the energetic cord that has kept us attached to the past hurt. It means we release its hold on our emotions so our focus can be free to be channeled into the present. It does not mean we have to accept harmful behavior or reconcile our old relationships. It doesn't mean we allow the abuse, we accept the abuse, or we think the abuse doesn't matter anymore. It doesn't make the past behavior okay. It makes us okay enough to move forward from the past behavior.

The more we think about, focus on, or fantasize about the past event, the more we keep it alive within us. Forgiveness isn't about saying it didn't happen; forgiveness is about stopping it from happening again and again within you.

Moreover, as you move into higher environments, it will become easier to let go of events that hurt you. It might take awhile, it might take conscious work, or it might take spending some time in grief for a while. Either way, it's possible to move into better-feeling places, regardless of what you've been through.

When we don't know healthier ways of easing the lower environment emotions, we use self-destructive ways like overeating, alcoholism, drugs, or smoking cigarettes instead. We can become addicted to the ease they bring us, which makes us less likely to want to work on those issues because we have found a temporary ease.

If we are trying to lose weight, we can't shame ourselves into doing it. Shame will make us want to eat more because food is comforting. Eating food is a form of ease exercise that we do to move up into better-feeling environments. That's why we only overeat when we're looking for ease in depression, shame, guilt, boredom, or anxiety. We can't use any of those feelings to motivate weight loss because they promote overeating.

If we want to change self-destructive habits, we have to find alternative exercises that give us the same feelings of ease. Then, we won't feel the need to use the habits that hinder wellness in our bodies. We won't even feel the desire for them because in a higher environment, they are not attractive or desirable. We don't even need to actively resist them. We simply don't want them anymore. It becomes that easy.

We eat differently in each environment. We have sex differently. Our marriages are different. Our relationships with our children are different. We make different choices based on where we are in the moment.

How we deal with things is largely due to where we are emotionally standing when we look at them. This is why it's important not to make decisions from lower environments. The results we receive when we act from anxiety or aggression are drastically different from the results we receive when we act from hope or joy.

We may not see it the same way once we feel better. In fact, most everything we do in lower environments is simply to make us feel better and move us up. The activities tend to be temporary in nature because they only look good to us when we feel bad. When we commit to something from those lower environments, they rarely last long.

This happens in relationships, as well. People say "yes" from lower-feeling environments and then don't want the relationship anymore after feeling better. They begin the relationship out of loneliness and then change their minds because their feelings have changed. This often leaves the other person feeling used or discarded. It also happens with purchased items—also known as buyer's remorse. You believe you want something, only to change your mind later. However, people don't really change their minds; they change their feelings, and then their minds change.

Once we have moved into another emotional environment, we will see everything in our lives differently. If we dip down into depression, we might not like anything we liked before. We might not feel love for the people we loved. We might not feel passion for our jobs anymore. The emotional environment changes the way we view our lives. It changes our behavior toward people and things.

As we practice emotions, we carve out emotional pathways between emotions that make it easier to transition from one to another. Jealousy might immediately trigger rage for you. It might trigger depression for someone else. Or jealousy might immediately trigger hope that you, too, can have that. Where we go after a particular emotion depends on what we've practiced. It depends on our emotional pathways and energetic momentum.

We don't always climb emotion by emotion in an orderly way. We jump, we dip, we skip, and we fall. We are usually jumping all over the place based on how often we practice the jumps and dips. Only you know your map. It may not be a straight line; it might be a zigzag. Either way, understanding the emotional environments will help support you as you try to navigate through your feelings.

Our emotional environments are important to the quality of our lives. To do better, we have to feel better. This book will help you understand the energy of your emotions and how they work in your life.

The following pages are created as a guide to emotional energy. You are welcome to use what works for you and to ignore what doesn't. Come back to it when you feel better, see how you like it then. Read it when you're angry, see how you feel then. If a particular chapter doesn't feel good, come back to it when you feel differently. Explore. Allow it to show you your emotional patterns and habits. It will bring up emotions within you. Allow it.

The Energy of Emotions

We will explore all ten emotional environments, along with each individual emotion associated with them. We will also explore the energy of the emotions and what they attract into our experiences. If you're mainly in an environment of anger, you will attract a type of person into your experience very different from an environment of joy. All circumstances, events, and people are pulled into our experiences based on our emotional environments.

Each environment will be broken down into four sections: the energy of that specific environment, what it attracts into your life, the thought clusters associated with it, and what you can do now to ease yourself.

Depending on in which emotional environment you are when you read through Part I, you might find yourself getting upset or finding relief. If you are in hope and you are reading about depression, it might not feel as important. If you are in depression and reading about joy, it might not feel at all possible. If you're nowhere near the emotional vicinity of the environment, you'll experience it differently. It might not resonate with you at all. You might even feel bored and want to jump through the sections.

My suggestion is that you read through the first part once just to get an understanding of the environments. They are all connected to each other, and to better understand one, you must understand the others, as well. You are welcome to come back to any specific environment later and review it again if you so feel the need. It's up to you. However you choose to read this book is perfect.

We experience all of these environments regularly. It can be for a moment, for a few hours, or even days. No one is ever stuck in any environment; however, we do create home environments with emotions in which we feel the most comfort. So while you may identify closely with one or two environments, you have and will experience them all.

You're welcome to take your time with this book. It will make much more sense if you take breaks and reflect on the links between past experiences and emotions. Or even notice those that are currently happening within your life.

My intention for this book is that it helps you find ease and relief, regardless of what you're feeling. May it uplift you into better-feeling environments.

Environment 1:
The Black Holes
Depression, Disempowerment, Despair, Grief

The Energy of The Black Holes:

Emotions dictate our current state of internal harmony. If the energy within us is flowing in concurrence, then we'll feel more positive emotion. Once we introduce resistance through thought, we begin to feel negative emotion, and then the energy begins to slow. The stronger the negative emotion, the stronger our resistance to the natural flow of energy.

The slowest energetic flow is in this environment. This is the heaviest emotional environment. It feels as if the weight of the world is on our backs. We feel as if there's a brick on our chests and we can't breathe. Even thinking and feeling is painful. Life is the hardest to live from this environment because there is very little energetic flow. Life *is* energy, so when it slows down as much as it does in this environment, it can feel as if we're actually not living. We can feel like zombies.

All negative emotions are varying degrees of resistance that slows down energy flow. It can be resistance to emotions, resistance to thoughts, to life, to events, to people, to work, etc. The stronger the resistance, the more powerful the negative emotion.

Depression is a cocooning experience. Once the energy slows down, we withdraw because life requires more energy than we have or can give. To put it simply, we are exhausted from the resistance we put up toward life, and we don't have enough energy to move out of it.

Maybe we are tired of fighting our thoughts, our feelings, the way we look, how others feel about us, the job we hate, the spouse who doesn't care, the money that isn't enough—everything. Maybe we can't see another way out of any of it, so we resign. We pull into ourselves.

This is the environment that is created after exhaustion from maximum resistance. It makes us want to give up the struggle we feel in the nearby environments, which are full of guilt, shame, victimhood, aggression, anger, or disappointment. We feel as if we can't possibly win over our heavy emotions, and so we stop living for the most part. We stop living so we can stop feeling.

We give up because everything pushes back against our resistance and exhausts us. Life becomes a battle. Everything feels like a tiring uphill climb, even simple things like chores around the house or going to the grocery store.

Resistance continuously pulls us down into lower environments until we hit the very bottom, which is this environment. It is like the deepest and darkest part of the ocean.

To go further with the analogy, if we were a body floating in water, then the more resistance we felt, the more we would sink. But our natural state is to float up to the surface where there is air and sunshine. And when we stop struggling and fighting within ourselves, we can naturally move up to the surface.

We can do some activities to help us intentionally move up faster, similar to swimming upwards, but ultimately, all we have to do is just let go of what weighs us down and we will naturally float up. It may be a slow process, it may take more time, and it might even feel like we're drowning sometimes, but we should never discourage whatever progress we're making, regardless of how slow it feels.

We come down into this environment because we're looking for some peace from all the resistance we feel. We want some form of relief and don't know how to get it. This is why so many people choose to give up completely in this environment and end their lives. They don't really hate their lives; they hate the feeling of resistance in their lives. They want to stop fighting. They are exhausted.

No one commits suicide over events, things, or even other people. We do it because we feel tired of all the shame or despair or grief. We do it because we can't stand to feel any longer. We do it because we can't imagine another way forward and we feel stuck in despair.

It is always the emotion we want to stop or end, not our lives. We are really looking for relief from the resistance. All we see is the bottom of the water and can't imagine how we would possibly move up. The more we focus on that, the more weight we add. It feels too dark and too much of a climb up. Just thinking about it feels exhausting.

Resistance makes life feel harder and heavier. All the things that used to feel easy and light now feel like a constant fight for our energy. It's resistance to resistance that adds more weight and keeps us at the bottom.

The more resistance we introduce into our emotions, the more we want to resign deeper into depression. The deeper we resign, the more we judge ourselves on what we "should" feel or do.

We can stay in this cycle for years. We can become very comfortable in this environment because it doesn't require much from us. It then becomes a lulling experience, a slow drowning. Except we never die. Our lungs fill with water and we feel like we can't breathe, but it won't end.

Since the energy is the slowest moving in depression, it can feel like a better alternative than the nearby environments of push-and-pull aggressive energy. There is still some aggressive energy here, but it is mostly directed toward resistance, which only feeds itself.

It can feel disempowering because it loops on itself. We fight resistance with resistance and make it bigger. Then, we notice how big it has become and we continue to respond the same way. We introduce more resistance through judgment and avoidance and keep it going until we exhaust ourselves.

Depression generally gives off the vibration of "stay away." We tend to be so far down in the dark water that others can't even see us. And when they can see us, they don't know what to do with us.

When we are depressed, we tend to isolate ourselves from everyone else. This usually ends up feeding the depression because social interaction can become a much-needed distraction that could help us float. We also don't like physical activity very much, even though becoming physically active can change the chemistry of depression and bring back some of our desires for activities.

Being outside in general, near nature, is an effective way to slow down the momentum of being depressed. There is no resistance in nature. Everything is free flowing. The sun doesn't strain to shine, the grass doesn't race to grow, and the grapes aren't in a competition with the apples for size or taste. But when we feel depressed, the last thing we want to do is go outside or see other people. And so the energy continues to feed itself.

Most of the time, when we're depressed, we just want to keep to ourselves and overthink about our lives. We end up feeding the energy of depression and prolonging the process of moving up into higher environments.

Each day begins to feel like the one before it, and the next thing we know, years have passed. Then, that acknowledgement of time passing can cause even more depression because we begin to judge our lives and feelings. We tell ourselves we've wasted our lives. We hate our past and can't see much of a future. We feel more hopelessness because we think it's never going to end.

Once depression becomes our home emotional environment, then we will find it easier and easier to come here. When events and circumstances are not to our liking, we can easily become depressed. It can become an emotional habit. Our response to life is to become depressed about it. The more we do it, the easier it becomes to get depressed.

There's a form of grieving attached to depression, almost as if we're grieving for our lives. Perhaps it's for the life we want but feel we can't have. Perhaps it's for a life we had but feel as if we lost it. Maybe we're grieving for the father we never had, or the mother who never loved us properly. Maybe we're grieving for a childhood that never happened.

Depression can be repressed grief, or it can be repressed anger. There's something that wants to be felt but isn't being allowed. Something is being resisted, and it's exhausting us.

Depression can also be compared to a Black Hole in the universe. The opposite of depression is joy (Environment 10) and the opposite of a Black Hole is a sun, radiating warmth and giving life.

A Black Hole forms when a beautiful radiating sun collapses in on itself and creates a powerful gravitational pull that sucks all of the light into an endless darkness. Anyone who has ever been through depression can confirm the feeling of that description.

Black Holes also have an event horizon, known as a point of no return. Anything that crosses the event horizon can never return. Depression can feel the same way. When we're in it, it can feel like there is no return from it. And that feeling perpetuates the depression because depression is a notorious liar. It will tell us lies about ourselves and the world around us in such a truthful sounding way that it can convince us that it can't or won't ever get better.

Black Holes don't just suck in their own light but also whatever light is around them. Depression and despair can suck the fun, joy, and ease out of everything that once felt great. Our hobbies can feel like chores. Work can feel like death. Our family can feel like effort. Everywhere we go, it can feel like we're in the wrong place.

Anyone within the emotional vicinity of depression is likely to get sucked in, as well. Someone from

Environments 2, 3, or 4 can easily get pulled into depression. The closer we are to Environment 1, the easier it will be to dip into it.

The next environment is victimhood, and so it's easier for someone who feels like a victim to dip down into depression than an annoyed person from Environment 6. Someone hopeful (Environment 8) is more likely to be disappointed (Environment 5) than depressed (Environment 1).

Where we go emotionally will depend on where we're used to going. If depression feels like a safe emotional environment, then we will come here whenever we experience something unwanted or unexpected. If it's easy to feel depression, it just means we've been practicing the feeling of it for a while.

The great news is that we can practice better emotional pathways and strengthen the ease with which we go there. If depression is currently your home environment, don't be discouraged. No emotion is a permanent state. Everything can be shifted and eased with the right practice and exercise.

When an emotion becomes a habit, it doesn't take much to trigger it again. If you've ever experienced any other emotion, you have some form of habit practiced in it. That means you have habits in hope and joy and love, as well. You can find them again, and you can strengthen them.

I've practiced more than a decade of depression and would become depressed at the slightest comment from someone else. Sometimes, they didn't even need to say anything; a look was enough. But I was able to strengthen better emotional habits, and so can you. All it takes is a little practice and a little belief that it's possible.

What it Attracts:

Depression is a bit different from the other environments because it's not a very active energy. This type of numbing or lulling emotional environment creates on the slowest level because it uses the least amount of energy. It tends to bring life to a standstill. Years can pass, and we'll still feel the same. There is little activity created in this environment. It's just the same type of day over and over again.

Depression can be a harbinger of illness because depression is a form of repression. We repress and numb emotions we would rather not feel, and that creates illness in the body. The more we resist or resign from our lives, the more that energy creates illnesses that help us continue to resign from life.

The activities that support us in staying balanced and healthy, like sunshine, exercise, better nutrition, social events, etc., are often the last things we want to do when we're depressed. So not only does the energy create illness, but so can the habits we establish in this environment. It's an energetic match, and that's why we don't "feel" like doing the things that keep us healthy.

Most people who are depressed feel as though they have no control over their lives. Illness feels the same way. They attract each other because they have similar energies.

Some people become ill, and stay hopeful that they will become well again, and some people become ill and then resign from life. The same illness can be experienced in different ways, which will create different outcomes.

It may seem hopeless at first, but depression is one of the easiest environments to move up from. There is nothing below it, we can only go in one direction: up.

If we don't continue to feed depression or loop ourselves back down when we're naturally moving up, it will easily relax and move us up. We don't move up by resigning and resisting; we move up through ease and acceptance. They are different energies.

Thought Clusters:

This environment is likely to compound a certain cluster of thoughts. One thought will trigger another like it, and that will trigger the next. We can spend minutes or hours thinking these types of thoughts, which feeds the energy of the environment. We rarely ever just think one of these thoughts—that's why they're called clusters. They usually pull each other into the thought process and are never isolated.

Thought clusters in the Black Hole can be exactly or similar to the following:

"What am I doing with my life?"
"Every day feels the same."
"Nothing ever goes my way."
"Why does everything have to be hard?"
"Nobody understands me."
"Nobody loves me."
"No one ever listens to me."
"No one cares."
"I wish I were dead."
"What's the point of life anyway?"
"Everything feels bad."
"What's the point?"

Thoughts in the Black Hole tend to be dark in nature. They focus around how unhappy we are, how much we don't like ourselves, how much others don't understand us, or how much things aren't working. There are few opportunities in this environment for hopeful thinking.

Hope is too high and too far of a jump if there is no practiced momentum for it. Most avenues out of this environment either circle the thoughts back into this environment or move us up into shame or rage, which eventually bring us back down here.

Former passions and hobbies might feel like effort or feel draining. We might find ourselves not feeling much love for ourselves or for others. We probably won't want to do much of anything with them.

This lulling state can create matching thoughts that continue to compound the emotion. Noticing how much we don't want to do things will pull in more thoughts about how much we don't want to do things. Then, we start to think about how we might never want to do things again.

They're all similar thoughts or thought clusters. And we can spend hours and hours with these types of thoughts. Thoughts feed the emotion, which creates similar thoughts, which continues the emotion.

There must be an interruption in the cycle of thinking and feeling. We will either have to consciously ease into another emotion or trigger one.

What To Do:

So how do you move up from depression? The answer depends on how long you've been in the environment and how much momentum you've built here. If you've been in the feeling of depression for a long time, then you will have to do something differently from someone who dips in and out depending on the subject.

If you dip in and out depending on the subject, the easiest way to move up is to place your attention on something that feels better. Which subject brings you relief? It could be writing, drawing, your dog, your kids, or anything that generally feels good.

Once you move your emotion up using other subjects, you can return to the depressing one from a better place, and then move that one up.

When you feel better, you remember that you've been through worse things and you made it out. You remember that there are plenty of people in the world who have been through worse. There are people who have gone from bankruptcy to millionaire. There are people who have recovered from cancer. It's possible to work through this issue. You've worked through other issues before.

When you approach the issue from a better-feeling place, you can move it into hope and optimism easily. If you try to tackle it when you're depressed and hate your life, it's going to be an uphill struggle that will most likely end with you crashing back down into depression. You can't "try" your way out of depression. You have to move the depressed feeling into another one.

So if it's one or two subjects, distract the current emotion by going to a better emotional place through another subject.

Go for a walk, meditate, play with a dog or a child, watch a funny movie, go to the gym. Find a way to get your mind off of the subject and on to one that feels better. It doesn't have to be joyful, but it has to feel better than depression. Somewhere around hope is your best stance. Then, better choices and answers will come to you.

Once your mind is more relaxed, you will start seeing the issue from better perspectives. Maybe you'll remember someone who has been through it and could have the answers. Maybe you'll see an ad for a seminar or a book that deals with that issue. Somehow, when your mind is relaxed and your energy is calmer, the answer will find its way into your awareness.

However, if you're overall depressed and have been for a while then the previous suggestions won't work for you as easily. The easiest and fastest way to move up from here is to get angry. It may be all you can muster right now. That may be the only place you can go other than depression.

How do you feel about me saying that depressed people are like Black Holes who suck the life out of everyone around them? Pretty upsetting, yes? It's kind of rude, isn't it? Maybe even offensive?

It doesn't matter what makes you angry as long as you begin to feel some movement. What do I know? I don't know your life. You probably have a really good reason for being depressed. You're welcome to throw this book across the room. Slam it down to the ground and stomp on it.

Take out a notebook and scribble RAGE across the front page. Make a list of all the people who have ever upset you. Write them angry letters in the notebook. Tell them off. Blame them for your life. Every time you feel depressed, shift it to rage. Move the energy. Don't let it become reenergized in depression. Create some energetic diversity.

Put on some angry music. Get yourself worked up. Take that anger to the gym or a punching bag. Go for a jog or a run. Do something physical to get the emotion and energy moving.

If you find that anger doesn't come easily. If you find yourself unable to move from Environments 1 to 3, then move to a place of allowing. The process of allowing will help ease the resistant energy.

Make a conscious choice to move into a more allowing state little by little. Find relief in allowing your emotions first. Do NOT resist your depression or grief. What you are feeling is real. It's not in your head. It doesn't make you a bad person. You're not doing it wrong. Don't fight your emotions. The more you fight or shame them, the longer you'll stay in this environment.

Acceptance is a form of allowing. Allowing is the opposite of resistance. Anything that we feel resistant toward will feed what we are resisting. We often think that resistance is keeping us safe because we're pushing something we don't want away from us, but pushing is directing energy. By focusing on what we don't want, we feed it our energy. Pushing away your depression only makes it more permanent.

Resistance attracts more of the thing we're resisting. The more we don't want to be depressed, the more we will be. We have to become relaxed and easy with it. We have to accept our depression for what it is — a cocooning experience — and not judge ourselves for it. The more relief we find in it, the easier it will be to move up. Allowance is the answer.

If someone wants to give you a compliment, allow the compliment. Don't resist it, don't negate it, and don't argue against it. If someone wants to offer you love or support, allow it.

If you can't start there, start smaller. Allow the warm cup of tea. Allow the comfortable bed. Allow the sinking feeling in the pit of your stomach. Accept and allow your present feelings and experiences. You might not like them because they're not what you want them to be but allow them as they are. In other words, don't hold resistance to them in your body. Breathe into your clenched muscles, breathe into the knot in your stomach. Breathe and allow. After that, if you want to change something, do it. But don't do it until you breathe into the present moment and allow it to be as it is right now. Resisting it doesn't change it; it changes your energy by creating disharmony. Accept then change.

Acceptance is the opposite of resignation. One has the energy of moving forward while the other is giving up. One is letting go, the other is quitting. Depression can make you resign. Even toward your own depression. Try accepting it first. Allow your depression. Feel the relief of that.

You don't have to fight your depression; you don't have to fight your grief. You don't have to fight anymore. It's okay to accept your feelings as they are. You're not a bad person for feeling them. You didn't fail as a human being.

While it may not be what you want, and you might not be where you wanted to be, you're moving in the direction of what you want, and that is great! You've taken an emotional step! Hurrah!

Find thoughts that make you feel better. They will inspire you into action that will continue to make you feel better. You might get the urge to go outside or call a friend. It can be anything, and as long as it's being inspired by better thoughts, it will lead to actions that feel better. It could even be putting on a sitcom and laughing for thirty minutes. You'll feel better for a moment. Then, you can continue to do things that feel better and slowly build momentum. Don't discourage any progress, regardless of how small it is.

If painting makes you feel better, do that. If running makes you feel better, do that. As often as you can, shift the focus off of whatever it is that reminds you of depression. Take a walk, go look at some flowers, sit in the sun, do something else. And once you find what works, try to do it at least once a day.

What we're not looking for in this environment is a complete jump into joy; that might be impossible. What we're really looking for is some movement up through relief. We want the energy to begin moving into a better state so that we can begin to heal what caused our depression or grief.

You won't turn around completely in one day, but you'll feel a little better. And that is an energetic shift. The more you shift, the more momentum you can build in that shift. Then, it will become easier and easier. It might take a while, but it will move you into another emotion where you can continue your progress.

All we're doing is looking for relief in this moment. If you can find relief now, and you can keep finding relief now, then you can move up from depression because now is all that exists.

Acknowledge the shifts. Acknowledge the positive thoughts. It's great and wonderful and perfect, and you should feel proud of yourself for doing it!

If you were just thinking, "I can do that," then congratulate yourself! That was a hopeful thought! Even if you're not in depression, a hopeful thought is always great!

When you notice and say things that feel truthful and hopeful, you feel better. "I can do that," feels much better. There are ways out of depression. Others have done it. You've probably done it, as well, a few times. You can do it again. It's possible. That's a true statement. There should be no resistance in that sentence if you feel hopeful. Your body should feel ease with it. There should be no tension accompanying those words.

Saying something that is true feels better than saying something you want to be true but you know it isn't. There will always be resistance and tension in those statements. To feel ease with it, you must believe it. You may not be done with your own personal depression, but you are done with depression in this book. That's one small accomplishment. That's where we begin. One becomes two and three and so on. Small steps are how it works.

How does it feel to have finished that chapter? A little better? Fantastic. Now, let's move on to the next environment.

Environment 2:
The Victims
Anxiety, Shame, Guilt, Insecurity

The Energy of The Victims:

 The energy of this environment is directed inward, as opposed to the energy of the aggressors, which is directed outward. Both have similar energies; the difference is in the focus.

 Both victims and aggressors will feel powerless, out of control, insecure, and vulnerable. Both will feel the need to do something about the way they feel. The healthy course of action will lead the victim to process their anger, deal with their feelings of vulnerability, and find strength in overcoming obstacles. The victim will come out stronger, wiser, and no longer thinking of themselves as a victim. They will find empowerment from their circumstances.

An unhealthy course of action for the victim will lead them to become an aggressor who victimizes others. They will not process their emotions, not accept their anger, and they will act as an emotional volcano that creates carnage everywhere they go. We've all known someone like that who is angry all the time and takes it out on the people around them.

An aggressor will also have anxiety, shame, guilt, and insecurity. The difference is that they will take that out on others, creating more victims. They will project their insecurities onto the outside world.

What makes one victim healthy and the other unhealthy? The willingness to accept and process their emotions. The more we repress, the more likely we are to victimize others. This doesn't necessarily mean we will become physical with them. We can victimize others emotionally and mentally. We can victimize others through betrayal, through lies, through manipulation. We can victimize people every day and not even realize it.

This environment requires self-reflection, self-healing, self-care, and self-awareness. It might also require boundaries and self-protection. Anger can be a healthy step forward from this environment. It's natural for us to become angry with others or with our circumstances when we are here. It's a natural movement up.

The first two environments lack self-importance and self-value. There's only so much we can take before we explode into a rage and move up to the next environment of the aggressors where we demand what we've been lacking.

Rage is a natural trigger to feeling undervalued. It's so easy to trigger when you have been abused, shamed, mocked, or taken for granted. Suddenly, you want your presence known and felt. You want your feelings acknowledged right now. You demand the respect you haven't been receiving. Unfortunately, it is likely that we will create more victims through our rage. It needs to be expressed and released. It must be done appropriately.

Shame, guilt, and insecurity are emotional states we take on from early experiences with others. Perhaps we lived in a household where we were neglected, constantly shamed, or told we weren't good enough. Perhaps our ideas were belittled, our feelings ignored, or our needs disregarded. Either way, we were unintentionally taught low self-worth. These early experiences have made it easier for us to dip into this environment.

We might find an interaction to be damaging while someone with a healthier self-esteem might find it to be normal. Our experiences with the world at large take on different meaning when we are here.

The first two environments are disempowering. This environment is higher than depression because fear is more powerful than numbness. We begin to feel, which begins to move the energy more.

Depression and anxiety both pull energy inward toward the self, which can feel overwhelming. When we are depressed and anxious, we become very sensitive to the energy of the people around us. We hold in more energy than we release, and so we feel more uncomfortable around others.

We might need to isolate ourselves and spend more time alone because we don't know how to handle all the energy that we are experiencing from others. It can feel exhausting, which might make us want to resign into depression.

The first two environments tend to go hand-in-hand. We often loop between them. In fact, sometimes, it feels like we're in both at the same time, having one foot in depression and one foot in anxiety or guilt. We might even feel fear in moving up from these environments because we feel comfortable here. Anger or rage might feel too far away from us. So much that if we ever find ourselves in those environments, we might frighten ourselves back into anxiety or we might shame ourselves back into victimhood.

We might also become people-pleasers in this environment because we believe that pleasing others will make us feel better and change our own energy. Since we are sensitive to other people's energies, we want to change them so we can feel good by default. This is a type of "borrowing" of energy, where we use the conditions around us to feel good and create better energy within us. Even though it might work, it is short-lived and we begin to depend on others to make us feel good.

True empowerment comes from not being dependent on the conditions, which is extremely hard to do in this environment. When we've been the victim of something, one of the things we learn on a subconscious level is that we can't be trusted. We can't trust our emotions, our instincts, our judgments, or our choices. We question ourselves all the time so we depend on others for emotional security, for answers, for the right course of action.

We're left constantly wondering if we're going to make a mistake that will cost us a lot and lead to a lot of pain. So it's easy in this environment to become dependent on others. It's easy for us to become people-pleasers. This, unfortunately, opens us up for more victimization. People will use that for their own selfish benefits.

People-pleasing doesn't work very long because it's a conditional energy and can shift in a moment. We either end up exhausting ourselves trying to please everyone or we open ourselves up for being used.

People-pleasing is a form of manipulation because we attempt to control how others feel, even if we're trying to make them feel good. We want to alter the conditions around us so we can create better energy within us. We want other people to act better so we can feel better when we look at them. We place the responsibility of our feelings on other people. We may want them to feel good or receive some kind of benefit, as well, but it's ultimately about our own anxieties and need for relief.

If we're pleasing other people so that we feel pleased ourselves, we're eventually going to be disappointed, angry, or depressed. Since our energy is conditional and borrowed, it won't be able to last us very long. We'll either end up blaming them or ourselves for our negative feelings.

We'll drain ourselves back down into depression because we'll begin to again feel not good enough. Our efforts will feel not good enough. It will seem like no matter what we do, other people still aren't pleased enough. The energy doesn't last. So we make that mean we're not good enough. This mirrors our insecurities.

Environments 1 and 2 are draining environments. There is no balance of energy and no free-flowing give and take, so it leaves us feeling exhausted. And as we become exhausted, we might feel guilty for not wanting to be around others anymore. We might even feel shame for being sick. We might begin to withdraw again and resign, creating more feelings of shame and guilt.

Shame and guilt are slightly different from each other but are similar energies. So are anxiety and insecurity. These four emotions are grouped together because they are in the energy of fear and victimhood.

Since the energy is withdrawn into the self and the fear is focused on the self, we tend to abuse ourselves in our own minds. When something occurs, we blame ourselves and feel shame again. We shouldn't have trusted, we should have known it was a lie, we should have stayed home, stopped at the red light, not said that, told our boss off, etc.

We feel shame again; we feel guilty or insecure. We don't want to be around other people again. We might even dip down into depression.

Even when anxiety feels like it's about other things happening outside of ourselves, it's still about the self. It still pulls in all the energy to the self. Anytime these four emotions are involved, it's pulling the energy into the self.

Our anxiety is about our lack of trust within ourselves to handle events, circumstance, or the outside world. It's about a lack of confidence or self-esteem in our abilities. We would almost prefer someone else to rescue us or take care of us. We don't feel adequate in making our own decisions. We might even feel anxiety around making simple everyday choices.

Shame, guilt, and insecurity are all about self-judgments and fears about not being good enough. The withdrawal of energy into the self creates a level of blindness. It narrows the focus away from everything else and directs it toward the self.

Anxiety and worry keep our minds on a loop that create more anxiety and worry. Even when we think we're worried about others, we're really worried about how we feel about others. We're worried about what we will have to say or do. We're worried about how much it will cost us emotionally, mentally, or physically.

Most fear comes from the anticipation of an event rather than the actual event itself. We worry beforehand as a form of preparation. We want to get ahead of our negative predictions. It's disguised as mental precaution when it's actually self-inflicted torment. The price of being ready for future suffering is that you suffer in the present moment. You fight the present moment in preparation for the future moment that may or may not happen.

That's not necessarily a bad thing. It's more of a survival thing. Because that's what victims do; they fight to survive. That's what happens in this environment. We are continually fighting to survive. We fight our thoughts, our emotions, our families, friends, co-workers, our bodies, the food we eat, our partners, the traffic; we are always in a fight for our emotions because we know that if we are to lose, we'll end up in the Black Hole again. We usually end up exhausting ourselves back into the Black Hole either way.

This is all normal when we're in the process of moving up. This is just one step in the process, and it doesn't have to be your energetic home. This energy is better than resigning. It's okay to worry about what we're going to do or how we're going to respond to things. It really only becomes an issue when we make it into one. That's when we begin to loop our emotions between shame and anxiety. We judge our emotions, and we make this our home emotional environment. We keep ourselves here through self-judgment.

We find ourselves here more and more frequently as we create momentum through our judgment. We don't allow ourselves to move up, and we just bombard ourselves with fear. We make ourselves a victim of our own minds. We turn our own energy against ourselves. We turn ourselves into a target.

All of our future experiences are being created through our current understanding and treatment of self. If we emotionally abuse or belittle ourselves now, our future experiences will hold similar experiences. *Then* will simply become more of the *now*.

You set the energetic tone for how others treat you by how you treat yourself. It doesn't get better until you treat yourself better. Since your decisions are made in the present moment, all that matters is how you feel right now. So it's important that you start feeling better right now. It's important that you take the time to take care of yourself now. You deserve it.

What it Attracts:

Environments 1 and 2 are creators of illness because energy is constantly being held in and not released as much. It's unbalanced and can create imbalance within the body. It can also lead to explosions of emotion, which would move us up one environment to the aggressors.

We might also want to isolate ourselves from others so we don't feel too much emotion/energy coming from them. We can become highly empathetic in this environment, which can make us weak and tired. It can feel overwhelming and overpowering at times.

Being around others can become too much for us to handle and so we often feel the need to continue to withdraw and isolate ourselves. Being in a crowded room can feel like too much energy.

However, the more we isolate ourselves, the more we perpetuate the energy of withdrawal, which loops us back into this environment, as well as the one below it.

Victimhood, however, is a different kind of powerlessness than depression. Depression is resigning energy, while victimhood is more active than that. We are more likely to take action from this environment than we are from depression. That is the crucial distinction.

Victimhood is not resigning. We may not like where we are, but we are more likely to do something about it. Even if we are to receive responses we don't like, we are still more likely to act.

However, both environments are similar in nature. So as a victim, we will continuously dip down into depression and then up into anxiety over and over again in a loop if we don't allow ourselves to move up into aggression. We have to continually move up until we reach better-feeling emotions.

Being a victim of something and staying in victimhood are two separate things. It's entirely possible to have been the victim of something or someone and still be living a joyful, passionate, or peaceful life.

The experiences that come from this environment can cause one of three responses: it will either move us down to depression and make us want to resign from life, keep us exactly where we are and amplify the feeling of victimhood, or move us up into aggression or blame where we will intentionally push out the energy. We might even go higher up into hope. It will depend on our momentum and which emotional pathways we have strengthened.

Since focus is the director of thoughts and therefore emotions, we can only shift our energy by shifting our focus. Begin small and ask yourself some questions. Which aspect are you looking at? How are you telling this story? Is it leaving you feeling empowered or disempowered? Is it draining you or revitalizing you? Are you inspired by it or made anxious by it? Even a small shift in perspective is enough to move you up in to a hopeful place.

When we feel like a victim, it can make us pull into ourselves and feel horrible about our actions or selves. This keeps us in a cycle of depression and shame. It can also make us rage and act out to get our power back. Where we go will depend on where we have built the most momentum.

If we allow the natural movement of our emotions, we'll get angry. It's very healthy for a victim to become angry. In fact, in most therapies, it's encouraged. It's a sign of natural movement up. It's a sign of healing.

However, so many times when we feel like victims, we shame ourselves back down into depression and disempower ourselves. We feel wrong for getting angry. Sometimes, we feel as though we deserved to be treated horribly and that it was our fault so we have no right to be angry.

Energy is about flow and ease. We can become joyful individuals easily, but we can also become depressed individuals easily. Where we go will depend on our energetic momentum and how much time we've spent creating it.

Momentum and energy are basically the same things. It is energy feeding more energy and creating more of the

Emily Maroutian

same. To shift, change, or alter what we have been attracting, we have to begin to direct our energy elsewhere.

That may not feel easy in this environment because Environments 1 through 4 can feel overwhelming with energy. It can feel out of our control. We might not even believe that we are the creators of our experiences. It can feel too farfetched.

For now, our best chance of getting to a higher environment that will make it easier to feel positive is to get angry. Anger will help us feel more in control of our lives and what happens to us. It will give us a sense of power that victimhood can't give us. It's a natural step up.

Thought Clusters:

This environment is likely to compound a certain cluster of thoughts. One thought will trigger another like it, and that will trigger the next. We can spend minutes or hours thinking these types of thoughts, which feeds the energy of the environment. We rarely ever just think one of these thoughts—that's why they're called clusters. They usually pull each other into the thought process and are never isolated.

Thought clusters in victimhood can be exactly or similar to the following:

"Why does this always happen to me?"
"Why does everybody hate me?"
"No one wants to talk to me."
"No one wants to help me."
"Oh, no; it's happening again."
"I can't breathe."
"What should I do now?"
"I feel so lost."

"Help."
"I'm afraid."

Thoughts in victimhood are also about the self. They mostly focus on how others have treated the self or will treat the self. Most of the thoughts lead to more shame, guilt, or anxiety.

When we see the world through this environment, we can only see the black-and-white battle between victim and perpetrator. This type of thinking creates more of the same type of thoughts. Soon, these feelings become habitual and easily triggered. We begin to see it all around us. We feel it all the time and become unable to function normally.

The types of thoughts we have in these lower environments loop us into the energy of them. The more we focus here, the longer we stay here. And the longer we stay here, the more similarly clustered thoughts form.

We can easily fall into a cycle of emotion creating thought, which creates more emotion, which creates more thought.

There must be an interruption in the cycle of thinking and feeling. We will either have to consciously ease into another emotion or trigger one.

What To Do:

This environment requires a lot of self-care and self-love. It requires that you put your needs before others. You have to consider what's best for you first. Don't put yourself in any position that will compromise your healing. If you do, anxiety will ring like an alarm letting you know it's time to leave.

Anxiety will force you to think of yourself first. It's no surprise that most people in this environment tend to be caretakers. They're people who place the desires, needs, schedules, or plans of others before their own. They're used to being there for everyone. They're used to draining themselves into illness.

This is why anxiety happens in this environment. Anxiety forces you to say no when you can't say it. Anxiety forces you to think about and care for yourself when you're not used to it. In some ways, it's a protector.

However, if we don't listen to what anxiety is trying to tell us about our assertiveness and self-esteem it'll expand out into various parts of our lives until we can't do anything without feeling anxious. It will debilitate us. Our protective tool will begin to harm us.

Rule number one in this environment, as well as the one before it, is: my needs matter. Say it to yourself often. Write it down on sticky notes and put it everywhere. It's okay for you to say no to friends and family. It's okay for you to take time for yourself. It's okay for you to think of yourself. You MUST.

Small shifts in this environment can create great ease. Doing some affirmations can help. Meditation, yoga, or Pilates can make you feel more in control of your emotions. Various types of martial arts also help. Aikido and Tai Chi balance our internal energies while also teaching us how to defend ourselves.

The answer might be therapy, it might be legal action, it might be the severing of a relationship, or it might be all of the above. Only you will know which action feels right for you. Just don't make yourself wrong for whatever you decide. This is about your healing, and the most important thing in this environment is that you begin to feel some level of control over your life and self.

You're welcome to choose rage, as well. Rage is a natural shift from anxiety, guilt, insecurity, and shame. When you're filled up with that level of emotion, you move the energy out quickly. There's a switch that happens. All that in-flowing energy just gets channeled out. It's a release. That's why it feels so good to let it out. This isn't the answer of course, but it's a step toward the answer. It's only a part of the process of healing.

A victim has every right to their anger. It's something that should be owned and accepted, not shamed and repressed. No one deserves abuse or mistreatment. No one deserves to be victimized. Anytime you blame yourself, you're going to shame yourself. Once you do that, you'll perpetuate the energy and slip right back down to a lower environment. It's better you become angry.

If it makes you feel powerful to rage, then take out a notebook and start ranting! Call up a friend and let them know you need a supportive ear for your rant. Go to a gym and start punching some bags. Go for a run. Work yourself up. Get angry and release the anger in a healthy way.

It's important that you find some relief. You can do that through ease and self-care, or you can do that through rage and release. Either way, take your power back. You deserve good things! You deserve to be treated with respect! You deserve love, too!

You deserve to be safe. You deserve to be healthy. You deserve a healthy and long life full of happiness and love. You deserve to have your needs met. You deserve to be listened to and respected. You deserve everything you wish for the people you love. That's self-care and self-love.

Why shouldn't you get to be the one who yells, too? How come everyone else gets to yell at you? You've got vocal chords! You've got energy and power, too! You are a powerful creator just like the rest of them. Who says you have to take anyone else's crap? That's anger.

Pick the route that feels best for you: self-care and self-love or anger. You're also welcome to do both. Give yourself some love and care while you get angry about the way others have treated you.

In this environment, you must do something because this is the environment that demands some kind of action for relief. It's important to link the relief with an activity you are choosing to perform. It's important to feel a sense of power come back into your life by linking your actions with your emotions.

Victims often feel like other people or events have the power over their lives and emotions, so it's important that you choose what you want to do to feel relief and that you give yourself credit for doing it.

However, some people don't feel comfortable feeling rage or aggression. It automatically makes them feel shame or guilt and dips them right back down into this environment.

If it feels better to find ease rather than to feel rage, you have to discover what puts you in ease. You can try some of the activities from the depression environment like walking or meditating or working on a hobby.

What activity makes you feel more at ease while also giving you a sense of control? Painting can do that, so can writing. Any kind of art or dance has that affect. You are in full control of what you create, and it's an easing exercise. It focuses your attention on your creation and distracts you from building more momentum in those other feelings.

If you have never done anything in art, it's a good time to start! Anyone can throw paint against a canvas; you don't have to be good at it. It's not about that. No one else has to see it or judge it. You can write words on paper; they don't have to be perfect. You can move your body to music; it doesn't have to look cool.

Practice taking your power back little by little through daily activities. You'll start feeling more confident about your emotions, and you'll find that insecurity and anxiety comes up less and less.

I've personally found the Emotional Freedom Technique (EFT) to be effective for worry and anxiety. It's often called tapping, and it involves using the tips of your fingers to tap on pressure points on the body to calm anxiety. These are the pressure points used in acupuncture and are very helpful in moving energy. They can also help interrupt the pattern of anxious thinking and reprogram your brain into calmer states. I've also used grounding exercises, as well as EMDR, Havening, and Somatic Experiencing. They are all effective for anxiety and even PTSD.

You can also try acupuncture or calming teas. It's really about what works for you. Experiment. See what you like. See what brings you ease. We're not looking for a 100% cure for these emotions. There is no such thing. You can't cure an emotion, but you can learn better ways of dealing with them. We want to find what works so we can use it again and again when we find ourselves in this environment. We want to build a momentum of ease.

We're really only looking for some movement up. You don't have to move it into joy yet. You don't have to feel good about it. Not yet anyway. Even if you can't completely move into hope, a little bit of movement is enough. Just a little bit of a shift is enough to keep you moving up.

Environment 3:
The Aggressors
Hatred, Rage, Revenge

The Energy of The Aggressors:

The previous two environments were disempowering. This environment, along with the next one, is about trying to gain more power and control over our experiences. While most of us can agree that acting out of this environment is not the most appropriate means of gaining empowerment, feeling within it is.

To be clear, feeling hatred for someone who wronged you, feeling rage and the need for revenge is normal. However, acting on it can be damaging, and depending on the act, illegal.

Every emotion is normal and healthy. It's the duration, the expression, and the meaning we give it that makes it unhealthy. It's not what you feel, but what you do with what you feel that determines its benefit and appropriateness.

All feelings are appropriate depending on the context of the situation. If you were victimized, it's appropriate to move into this feeling environment. It's appropriate to take the right actions in moving forward. It's not appropriate to victimize others, which is what can happen when we act out of this environment.

Can you go from depression and victimhood to confidence, healing, self-empowerment? Yes, of course. You don't have to stop by this environment. You can skip to understanding, forgiveness, and peace. However, most of us take this route because it feels emotionally easy. It's easy to go from feeling like a victim to feeling angry about it. It's also natural. You're not wrong for feeling it.

This is the environment where we feel as if we're gaining more control over our lives. Our energy becomes more aggressive, and we seek immediate results. We want actions, and we demand changes. This is where the energy begins to move faster.

The first two environments were about withdrawing energy into the self. It was slow moving and lulling. Environment 3 is about regaining power. This is the environment where the energy begins to move more. There is a lot of active force and aggression in this environment.

As aggressors, we are in very close emotional proximity to victims. We bump into each other often and switch roles with each interaction. Ultimately, we're both on the opposite ends of the same energy. This makes it easy to hop up and down.

For instance, your boss might yell at you and make you feel victimized. Then, you go home and notice the dishes haven't been washed and so you yell at your kids, victimizing them. Some of us drink alcohol because we feel we have been victimized by life, and in turn we end up victimizing our family members with our heavy drinking and out-of-control behavior. Perhaps your ex-partner cheated on you and now you're treating your new partner terribly because of it. You don't trust them or anyone else. You create arguments over small things that don't matter. You feel overall hostile, making them pay for someone else's mistakes.

There are countless examples of this kind of back and forth we do every day. If we are in this environment, then we often jump up and down to and from the one before it. Environments 2 and 3 are energetically interlocked. The only way to stop being one is to transcend both. Why both? Because to some degree, we are all both.

As I try to explain this environment using the pronoun "we," it becomes a difficult challenge because labeling ourselves as "victims," and then "aggressors" posses a language problem. I'm forced to use "they," which is impersonal, or even "you," which can feel aggressive, accusatory, and judgmental.

As I continue discussing this environment and use labels like "victim" and "aggressor," I want to make clear that we are both. There is no "other." I'm speaking about when WE feel like victims and when WE feel like aggressors. Even when I use "you," I am not singling you out specifically; I'm speaking to all the yous, including myself.

I will try to use "we" as often as I can to make it feel inclusive and personal because it is. This book is not about singling out any behavior or type of person and shaming them for their feelings. We are far more alike than we realize. We all have been both and will be again and again as we move onto different levels of understanding. Each new problem will pose a new tug of war in our perception of ourselves. It's the natural process of emotional growth and evolution. It's not wrong to feel anything.

My intention for this book is not to judge others or make them feel wrong for their emotional environments. I truly believe that anyone can feel better regardless of where they are now. Moreover, as they feel better, they will behave better.

No one is above anyone else when it comes to emotions because we've felt them all. We are all capable of the darkest of emotions and the highest of joys. We all feel the same feelings — we just act differently through them. So let's continue, and please keep in mind that we exist on both sides of the same coin.

All aggressors were once victims; this is why we stopped by this environment. We only become aggressors when we feel we have been betrayed, violated, hurt, or unjustly treated. Rage comes after a violation. Wounds trigger anger. No one in peace has ever fought with another. We would have to stop by victimhood first.

What happens with most aggressors is that we are shamed back down into victimhood and then we have to work ourselves back up into aggression again to regain some power over our lives.

When we, as victims, take matters into our own hands or take legal action, we become the aggressor. Even if revenge is legal and labeled as justice, it's still a power response to feeling like a victim. It's also a natural and appropriate step up from victimhood. Aggression is not wrong when it is appropriate.

To be clear, I am not suggesting that this process makes you a "bad" person. It's natural to move from victim to aggressor. Children do it all the time. No child becomes a bully unless they have been made powerless in another area of their life. A child gets picked on by an older brother at home, and so he goes to school and picks on a younger student. Perhaps the old brother is being picked on by the father or some older children at his school. Children behave this way automatically because it comes naturally from their emotions. To transcend it, they must be taught conflict resolution skills and appropriate expression of emotions. Without that, they will naturally stay in this environment and become lifelong aggressors.

I'm also not implying that this process is good or right. Good and right are judgments, as are bad and wrong. This is a process, and we all end up on both sides of this process because that's what it means to be human. The answer is not to stay in one environment or the other. The answer is to transcend them both. The answer is to continue to rise.

All aggressors and bullies are victims in pain who have turned the energy outward. Bullying a bully doesn't end bullying. It cycles it because the bully becomes the victim again, which gives them more pain to turn outward. They have no other choice but to come back through this environment again, victimizing more people.

Rarely do aggressors move up into alignment when others shame and punish them. They will either remain aggressors and feel justified, or they'll drop into victimhood, thus switching the roles. In which case, they'll have to move back up into aggression once again to regain power.

You might not care if an aggressor feels better. You might not want an aggressor to move into alignment—why should they get to feel joy after all they have done? Why should they get to be happy? Because happy people don't reoffend. We don't stop criminal behavior by punishing them into victimhood; we stop it by moving them up into better-feeling environments that don't inspire criminal behavior. We stop it by teaching, not punishing.

This doesn't mean that they won't have to answer for their choices. Self-responsibility is an important aspect of higher environments. You can't get to joy without being responsible for your own thoughts, emotions, actions, and choices. Joy doesn't happen to us, we create it.

If we punish aggressors back down into victimhood, they will continue the behavior. We want them to transcend the behavior, and that happens in higher emotional environments. We have to be honest with ourselves, do we want change or do we want punishment and revenge? How we answer that question will depend on which environment we're in at the moment.

People transcend through healing, through understanding, through support. People don't transcend through punishment, abuse, shame, or humiliation. The latter perpetuates the cycle of victimhood and aggression.

So often we would rather push others down into a behavior that feels more controllable and comfortable for us, like victimhood or depression, than to help move them up into an environment where aggression wouldn't be a possibility, like peace or joy.

This is also a testament to how we were raised as children. Punishment was the way others controlled our unwanted behavior. However, it's not effective. It just looks effective because the person dips into a lower environment and stops the aggressive behavior temporarily. Not because they learned a better way or a better behavior, but because they now feel depression or despair or unworthiness.

We shame children into "calming" behavior. But the behavior isn't calm; it's withdrawn. And it will only be a short time until they naturally move up and go through aggression once again. Next time around, it might be even more aggressive because now they have more pain. If we use the same methods again, we'll push them back down, and on and on it will continue in a cycle.

Aggression, generally speaking, is not a bad thing and does not need to be punished. It needs to be understood and eased when it first appears. No one becomes aggressive unless they feel they have been wronged in some way. We can look at the behavior and shame it, or we can look underneath the behavior and offer alternatives.

No one is wrong for feeling like they need more control over their lives and circumstances. It's only when we fall into cycles of shaming ourselves, and then raging against others, that we begin to create negative consequences.

We all do little acts of revenge from time to time. How many times have you delayed sending a response back because you were angry with someone? How many times have you said you won't go to someone else's party because they didn't come to yours? How many calls have you ignored because you secretly wanted to punish that person for something they said or did? How many times have you stopped yourself from complimenting someone because you didn't want them to "have" the compliment?

We do it all the time, and we do it in subtle ways. We do it by purposely being late or making an off-putting joke we know the other person won't like. We hide it behind sarcasm. We retract our attention from someone to punish them for retracting their attention from us.

We may not consider ourselves aggressors, but there are many different degrees of aggression. We can respond to others through little acts of punishment and not even realize it. We are constantly trying to adjust other people's behaviors through negative reinforcement because that's all we know. If the subtle acts don't work, that's when we get angry and magnify our response.

Rage can feel like a powerful emotion. Especially if we have been feeling powerless, shameful, or anxious for a while. Depending on where we were before, it can either feel liberating or horrible. If we were in depression or shame, then it will feel better because it's a step up. If we were in hope, it can feel horrible because it's a dip down.

Rage feels alive and powerful. We can't feel victimized or powerless when we are raging. We can't even feel anxiety when we're that fuming angry. It eliminates fear from our mind and instead focuses it on whatever is making us rage. This is why we rage—because it feels better than being a victim. It feels better than being afraid.

This environment of hatred, rage, and revenge is normal and natural in the wide range of human emotions. As long as we don't unpack and live here, it's okay if we're temporarily passing through. We all feel it, but we don't have to make decisions from it. Also don't judge yourself back into shame when you feel it. You'll get stuck in a loop.

So many times when we naturally move up into rage, other people can shame us back down into fear or depression because we are easier to manage there. People are much easier to handle in Environments 1 and 2 than in 3 and 4. Usually, the people around us will view our rage and anger and will try to move us back down through guilt or shame because we are less threatening there. A depressed person seems calmer than an angry one, but an angry one is higher up and therefore closer to peace. Depression is a false peace.

This type of guilt can cause us to think that we are bad people for feeling rage or anger. "Don't feel angry." "It makes you a bad person." "Don't rage like 'those' people." "I don't want to be like that." Other people's fear of our emotions can dip us back down into depression or shame. Sometimes, it's our own fear that dips us back down. We don't want to be like the people we knew growing up or have seen on TV.

We don't want to be the aggressors because aggressors are always labeled badly. According to society, aggressors are always bad people. This is why we prefer to lock them up in prison and forget about them, instead of teaching them how to move up in a more appropriate manner. We interrupt the natural emotional progress by constantly introducing shame into it and forcing them back down.

"You should be ashamed of yourself." It's best that they are not. Contrary to popular belief, shame doesn't stop the behavior; it only multiplies the energy, which will come out in another way later. So even if it might seem like the behavior has stopped, it hasn't. It's only been transferred into another area of their behavior.

Calming ourselves out of rage by becoming depressed isn't as productive as sitting with the rage and then naturally feeling the calm that comes after releasing it. Dipping down is a temporary course of action and will bring us back into rage again and again because we naturally rise and will have to move past that environment once again. We will face it again.

These emotions are common and they are healthy. As long as they are expressed and released appropriately, they pose no problem.

What it Attracts:

If we are moving through these emotions and we don't have much momentum in them, we won't create much of anything. We might pull in an experience or two, but if we don't judge it or shame ourselves for it, we will easily move up again.

We can notice ourselves trying to punish someone else for not calling us back or being late, and we can find some ease in the moment. We can learn to relax ourselves and let go of the little acts of punishment we inflict on others for not being what we want them to be.

We can learn to honor our feelings and manage them better. This will help us move through them in a healthy manner. The only time aggression begins to create reoccurring events and situations is when we fall into the cycle of victimhood and aggression and we don't allow ourselves to move up. We don't allow ourselves ease, and therefore we loop. Once it becomes a dominant energy, then we begin to attract more powerfully from here.

If we find ourselves frequently in this environment, we'll also find ourselves in victimhood a lot. Aggressors are really just victims (or feel like victims) who have found the relief of rage and control. But we must be careful here because we can easily feed what we don't want.

As the famous Nietzsche quote goes, "Beware that, when fighting monsters, you yourself do not become a monster... for when you gaze long into the abyss. The abyss gazes also into you." It's a very thin line between

Environments 2 and 3. Whatever we accuse others of doing to us, we can easily magnify in our own behavior.

We can end up raging at a raging man, hating someone who hates us, and perpetuating the energy of the thing we don't want. We can become the thing we feel angry about. As aggressors, we rarely feel as though our behavior is our fault or doing. It is almost always a reaction to others, which we blame for our reactions. This doesn't allow the energy to transform. It keeps us feeling stuck and turns us into what we don't want.

Hatred attracts more things to hate and more people who bother us. Rage attracts more things to rage against. Discrimination attracts more things to discriminate against. Hate and rage solve no problems, they only perpetuate them. They are not the answer; they are a temporary stop on the way to the answer.

Energy is the currency of the universe and when we "pay" attention to something we "buy" that experience. The more we focus on things that make us hate and rage, the more we amplify the energy of it in our experience. We repeat what we focus on and it becomes harder to let it go.

Think of your focus as a charger. It sends more power to where you channel the energy. You can charge up aggression, problems, and conflicts or wellness, compassion, and harmony. You can charge peace or war, love or hate, success or failure. You are the connecting factor between creative energy and reality.

By fighting something, we strengthen it because we use aggression. Aggression is mostly met with more aggression because they match. Being anti-war creates more wars. It's far more energetically effective to be pro-peace. Then you feed the energy of peace. The focus needs to be on what we want, not on what we don't want. We can't really focus on what we don't want and feel peace or love. We can't feel good about something that feels bad. So we have to work on focusing on the aspects that do feel good. The aspects we do have control over. That's how we magnify them. Focus on equality, love, harmony, peace, and joy. Amplify what you want instead of fighting against what you hate.

Energy flows to where our attention is focused. So even if we're looking at something and saying "no," or "don't," we're still feeding it because that's where our energy is focused. There is no "don't" in energy. If you think about one thing all day, your energy is going to be full of it, even if you hate it. You are going to become a beacon for that thing and you're going to attract it into your own experience. You cannot try to hurt others without hurting yourself in some way.

Hilter's main focus was a group of people (Jews) he believed were a threat to humanity. So he placed all of his energy into stopping them. What he ended up doing was creating a group of people (Nazis) who became a threat to humanity and they had to be stopped. The energy will always circle back on itself because while we think we're focusing it in one direction, we're really feeding something else.

Hitler, ultimately, received what he fought for. The threat to humanity was stopped. And by focusing on that energy, he became the threat to humanity that was stopped. He destroyed himself and his reign because his focus was on destruction. He fed the energy of rage and hate until it collapsed in on him. His hateful energy boomeranged back onto himself. We can't stand up against others without standing up against ourselves. Instead we must stand for love, peace, and compassion. We must perpetuate what we want. We must do it through the energy of progress and change, not destruction and hate.

Some religious family groups that believe in "protecting families" think that LGBT people are destroying families by getting married and starting families. So they fight against LGBT families and end up trying to destroy families in their effort to protect families. Most importantly, they don't even realize that they are doing the thing they are fighting against. So, ultimately, they are working against their own cause. Aggression has a way of circling back on itself.

This is how energy loops in on itself. We can't fight for peace. We can't destroy families to protect families. We can't take away other people's happiness to ensure our own. We can't bomb our way to safety. It doesn't work that way. The energy won't allow it. It only feeds itself.

By focusing on someone who we believe is the source of our misery, we become the source of our misery. By complaining about someone who complains, we become a complainer. By gossiping about someone who gossips, we become a gossiper, too.

Our focus will pull it into our experience every time. The more we are bothered, the more we ensure that we will continue to be bothered. We will feed the energy of the thing we hate until it grows so much that it's everywhere around us or until we become it ourselves. We can't fight energy; we can only feed it or withdraw it through focusing somewhere else.

Either way, energy is life. It is a life force and where we direct it is where we send more life. If we don't want to feed the energy of something, we must pull our attention off of it.

In this environment, we will find ourselves to be a victim still, but we will most likely push out our energy instead of pulling it in. This is once again a normal and natural process as long as we don't magnify it, act on it, and make it a home environment.

Thought Clusters:

This environment is likely to compound a certain cluster of thoughts. One thought will trigger another like it, and that will trigger the next. We can spend minutes or hours thinking these types of thoughts, which feeds the energy of the environment. We rarely ever just think one of these thoughts — that's why they're called clusters. They usually pull each other into the thought process and are never isolated.

Thought clusters in aggression can be exactly or similar to the following:

> "You're going to pay for this!"
> "Do you know who I am?"
> "Talk to me like that again, and I'll punch you."
> "Don't test me!"
> "You're going to be sorry."
> "I hate you!"
> "I wish you were dead!"
> "I'm going to kill you!"
> "You're sickening!"
> "I'm disgusted with you!"

Thoughts in rage and aggression generally pour out fast. There is no second thought, no filter to stop anything. We might say the most horrible things in this environment.

The thoughts and emotions are almost always focused on someone else. It can be directed toward the self, as well, but most of the time we seek revenge against others, we rage against others, and we hate others, even if we might secretly hate ourselves or our own lives.

If we view the world from this environment, we might find that people want to take advantage of us. They are always pressuring us or pushing us. We can easily find ourselves in battle with others. We are always striving for control over ourselves and our lives.

It can create a very aggressive emotional environment everywhere we go. We often become the source of our problems but are too full of rage or hate to see it. This environment can make us blind to other people's pain because we only respond from our own.

We can easily become locked in an environment of constantly needing to justify ourselves or our actions and emotions. This constant battle can create similar situations and therefore thoughts, which keeps us looping back into this environment.

It's very easy to feed the energy of an environment. If we allow the thoughts and emotions to cycle over and over again, we will soon find that years pass and we are still just as angry and without any hope for resolution.

There must be an interruption in the cycle of thinking and feeling. We will either have to consciously ease into another emotion or trigger one.

What To Do:

Revenge isn't necessarily bad. Artists can channel that energy into great revenge songs, paintings, books, and movies. We love watching, reading, and listening to them because it makes us feel better. It reminds us that no matter what happens to us, we can have some control over our lives and can prevail over our circumstances. It makes us feel powerful.

However, there is a significant difference between power and empowerment. The pursuit of power comes from denying and masking our insecurities because they make us look weak. The attainment of empowerment comes from embracing and understanding our insecurities and how they make us whole.

In this environment, you will feel as though you are gaining more control over your life, but you won't be able to feel true empowerment until you're in higher environments. In the meantime, take as much time as you need to feel what is demanding to be felt in the present moment. But keep in mind that all emotions are temporary reactions and they can't be sustained for long periods of time. Allow them to settle and rest without reigniting them through judgment or shame.

Feel the feelings, and then allow yourself to move up from them. There is no shame in wanting control in your life. If you want to partake in a revenge fantasy where you walk into a room with the most beautiful girl on your arm as everyone who has ever upset you watches on in jealousy, do it! If it brings you ease and relief, engage in that fantasy.

If you want to write letters in a notebook telling people how much they hurt you and how much you hate them, do it! If you want to make a hate list and write down all the people who ruined your life, do it! And then, write them letters in the notebook telling them how horrible they are.

Give the feelings of aggression the space they need to complete. We so often interrupt the process through shame and judgment. Allow them to pass through. Allow them to go.

If you want to move through the feelings of being an aggressor, you can do so without ever hurting or effecting anyone else. It's when we don't do something to release those feelings that we end up creating pain for others.

Instead of finding a healthy way of releasing the revenge fantasies we have, we act on them, creating tragedies, pain, and trauma.

It is natural to want revenge. It is natural to want to do something about a situation that doesn't feel good. But this is not the place from which to do it. When you find yourself in this environment, your first and only goal should be relief. Relief will move you up into environments that will help you make better decisions.

When you act from this place, you create more pain and victims. So the best action is to move the rage or hatred in a more healthy way. It's when these feelings compound and there is no relief from them that people become aggressors and predators. They act as a form of last resort just to finally find some relief.

You don't have to act on any of your emotions, but it's important that you really feel them. When you can feel the rage rising, stop for a moment and place your focus in your body. How does rage or hate show up in your body? Does it feel like clenched fists? Breathe into your fists and relax them. Does it feel like tightness in your throat, breathe into the tightness and release the tension. Find the emotion in your body, and breathe into it. This will bring you immediate relief.

It also helps to describe the feeling in terms of objects and colors. This will engage the creative part of your brain, which will help calm the fight-or-flight response. Does your rage feel like a volcano in your chest? What color is it? How does the lava feel? Is it contained or is it spewing? Does it feel like a ball of fire? Is it spinning? In which direction?

You can move through these emotions and get to a better-feeling place without ever involving others. You can breathe through your feelings, you can engage in a physical activity, like a walk or playing sports. You can write out your feelings in a notebook. Do what brings you relief, and then act.

I have also written a book full of soothing passages, empowering affirmations, and relieving exercises to help bring ease and relief to your mind and body. It will also help you learn grounding and mindfulness exercises for relief from heavy emotions. If you're looking for more ease, please consider reading *The Book of Relief*.

You don't have to feel guilt or shame for feeling rage or wanting revenge or feeling hate. You have access to these emotions because you're human. We all have a wide range of emotions we can feel throughout our days. It's just a matter of where we spend most of our energy.

Let the thoughts come without judging them, feel the relief, and allow yourself to move up. Once you're in a higher emotional environment, you won't be thinking those types of thoughts or feeling those emotions. Those thoughts won't even occur to you because they are a result of the emotional environment you're in now.

You will never think those types of thoughts in hope or joy because those emotional environments don't produce those thoughts. So the goal here is to experience relief from rage or revenge so that it will move you up. This can happen in a minute, in an hour, or a decade. That all depends on how much momentum you create in an environment by looping thoughts back to the perceived hurt.

So if you're feeling rage or hate or want revenge right now, don't shame yourself back down. It's okay to feel justified in them for a little while. This is you, taking your power back. It's a part of the process.

Be easy with yourself. You've been through a lot. It's okay for you to feel angry. It's okay for you to be upset about the things that happened to you. In fact, it's better that you feel angry about it than if you feel like you deserved it. It's healthy for your self-esteem to be angry about negative experiences. It's good that you feel angry that someone else treated you horribly. You do deserve better treatment. You deserve good things. You deserve to be happy, and healthy, and safe.

This book is not meant to create more shame in you. It's not created to make you hate your feelings or become worried about everything you think. Allow yourself to feel what you feel instead of getting mad at yourself for not feeling what you should feel. Think your thoughts instead of worrying about what you should be thinking. Claim your decisions, choices, desires, thoughts, and feelings. You are not yours until you allow all that you are right here, right now. That includes all of your emotions. Yes, all of them. The days of making yourself feel bad for feeling are over.

Feel some relief in that. You are in the process of taking your power back. That's a good thing! You are moving up! Take that aggressive energy and release it in a more healthy way. Find what works for you. Go swimming, running, play a sport, write it out. It's an active energy, and it wants action. Now.

Environment 4:
The Projectors
Anger, Blame, Jealousy

The Energy of The Projectors:

When we are in this environment, we also force our energy out onto others, but it is a much softer energy than rage, hatred, or revenge. There is a lesser urgency to act from this environment than in the one before it. It is softer.

Anger is much easier to control than rage. However, rage is just a small step from anger. We can very easily make the jump from being angry to a full-on raging fit.

Even though anger is a softer energy, it is still forceful. The focus is usually projected onto others, but we can also be angry with ourselves, as well. We can blame others, but we can also blame ourselves. Usually, when we feel angry with ourselves, we find another target to direct our anger toward because blaming others feels better than self-blame.

Much like the environment before it, the energy here also requires a release of some kind to find natural relief. Dormant anger can easily become rage, which is much harder to control. The energy wants to move, and if it doesn't find an outlet, it will explode into movement. The energy WILL find a release whether we choose to release it in a more natural and productive manner or just force it to explode in a fit of rage. Either way, it will move.

Blame is a form of releasing control over our lives, but at the same time, it is still an act of control. When we blame others for our circumstances, we take away the control we have over them. If we are not responsible, then we don't have the power to change or fix anything. But at the same time, by blaming others, we are starting to take more control over our emotions. It's energetic progress. It's not the most productive way to begin, but it's a beginning nonetheless, and as long as we don't stay in a perpetual state of blame, we can move on.

Most self-help books advise us against blaming others. However, a little blame is emotionally healthy, depending on where we are in these environments. It is a part of the natural process for our emotional wellness, and a little bit of it can create a lot of ease.

If blaming ourselves makes us feel depressed but blaming others makes us feel angry, then the latter is healthier. If, however, blaming ourselves makes us feel more in control and blaming others makes us feel disempowered, then it would be the opposite. It depends on each individual.

The only thing that we need to be aware of is that the relief we feel from blaming others can motivate us to do it repeatedly, thus becoming a habit. Once it does, we'll be practicing and creating from this environment daily, which will then become our emotional home environment. This means that our dominant experiences will be from this environment, which will continue to feed the emotion.

We will become projectors who assign the responsibility of our feelings and lives onto others and then blame them for what occurs in it.

In this environment, we will constantly look out from ourselves and try to find others to blame and be angry with. We will project our misery onto the world and feel as though everything and everyone else needs to be changed or fixed. We begin to believe that we would feel better if only others were better. If only circumstances were better. We give up the responsibility over our emotions. We become projectors of blame, anger, and jealousy.

Jealousy and anger tend to go hand in hand, but jealousy is a softer energy than anger. Jealousy is the softest emotion in this environment. But whether it is valuable will depend on the intensity of the emotion and, ultimately, where it is focused.

There is a hopeful jealousy and a hopeless jealousy. If we are looking at something we want but believe we can never have it, we are going to feel hopeless or maybe even angry about it. We might even hate the person who has what we want. It might make us cruel or bitter. We might start horrible rumors about them or even believe rumors just to make ourselves feel better. We might even wish for their downfall.

This occurs a lot with famous people. We become almost obsessed with how badly we think they're living their lives because it makes us feel better about our own. We feel smarter because we think we would have handled their lives or money differently. We judge them to bring ourselves ease.

If, however, we believe that we could also achieve or possess what we are jealous of, then we feel a hopeful kind of jealousy. It might make us put in more hours at work, start new projects, or change jobs. We might change our hair or appearance to feel better. It will set us into action that will bring some form of relief.

If we know we will achieve or possess it, then we skip jealousy all together and just go straight to excitement or eagerness.

For example, if we were planning a trip to Rome, have already bought our tickets, and were just waiting for the day to arrive, we would feel excitement if we met up with someone who just returned from Rome. It would make us more eager about our own trip. We would ask questions and request names of good restaurants. It would feel great, even though we were not in Rome yet.

If we wanted to go to Rome, had the money and time or could come up with the money and time, we might feel some hopeful jealousy. It might make us want to search the Internet for flights, hotels, or sightseeing locations. We might look at our calendars and wonder when we would be able to go, if we were to plan it. We might ask others about their experiences. We might start asking friends or family members if they would go with us. We begin to take small action steps even if we don't end up actually going.

However, if we wanted to go but didn't have the time or money and didn't believe that we could come up with the time or money, then we would feel a bitter or defensive kind of jealousy. We might tell others it's a bad time to travel. Everything is so expensive with the economy being down. I heard Italians are rude. What's so good about Rome anyway?

We begin to talk ourselves out of wanting what we wanted and then proceed to negate other people's positive experiences of it. We might not even continue listening to their vacation story. We might just change the subject to make ourselves feel better. We can't stand that other people have something we want that we believe we can't have. It can make us cruel or aggressive toward the other person.

All three scenarios take place in the same location; let's say it was a grocery store where we bumped into an old friend who just came back from Rome. However, all three scenarios take place in three different emotional environments. The first one will be in eagerness and excitement, which is Environment 9. The second one will be in hope and belief in the possibility of it, which is Environment 8. And the last one might be in any of the first five environments bouncing from depression to anger to pessimism to disappointment to jealousy.

Each emotional environment will change the way we experience the encounter. It will either leave us feeling more excited about our trip, hopeful and motivated to go, or upset and grumpy that we can't go. None of it will depend on the other person or the location. It will only depend on our own perception of our life and the possibilities within it.

The future — or better yet, our idea of the future — will affect how we feel now, in the present moment. We are not standing in Rome, we are not on our way there; we are in a grocery store, buying food. And yet, what we expect has a great deal of influence over our emotions.

If we allow our jealousy to make us angry and scornful of others, then we're dipping down into lower environments. This doesn't change their plans. It doesn't change how much they loved or enjoyed their trip. It only changes our emotions and energy, which affects our lives.

It's okay to envy others or to feel jealousy. When it turns back down into anger or revenge, then it's moving in the opposite direction. Then, we want to sabotage other people's emotions so we can feel better about our own. We become aggressors, trying to take something good away from others so we can feel better about not having it.

We might feel jealousy over our friend's romantic relationship and say negative things about their partner to create problems for them. We might even use the opportunity, while they're having problems, to add fuel to the fire and make things worse.

Once we feel a vengeful kind of jealousy, then we begin to destroy our relationships, which never makes us feel better. We might even blame them for our own vengeance.

Jealousy can blind us to our own cruel actions or words because we feel justified in it. We feel as if it is other people's faults that we don't have what they have. So we want to take it away from them. We want to ruin it for them. We want them to feel as horrible as we do.

However, there is also a productive form of jealousy or anger. It's when someone uses it as a fuel to do better in their own lives, instead of destroying other people's lives to feel better. There are many people who have created success for themselves while using jealousy or even revenge as energetic fuel. The best revenge, as they say, is success.

Jealousy can sharpen our focus and give us extra energy. It can help us find ways and means that were once unavailable to us. It can be beneficial if we use it right.

When we're in a higher emotional environment and we dip down into jealousy, it doesn't feel good. It might trigger immediate anger or blame and make it easier to stay in a negative state. However, if we were to move up to this environment, then it would be a softer feeling. There would be more ease in it. Jealousy after anxiety feels better than jealousy after hope.

Most of the benefits in the environments depend on the direction in which we're moving. A dip into the environment always feels worse than a climb into that same environment. The way we know the difference is through the amount of relief we feel.

Relief always means a rise, especially if it comes after negative emotion. It signifies a release of the energy, which is a very good thing. Even if we were in a negative emotional environment, feeling relief from there into another negative emotion is a rise. Moving from rage to blame is a rise.

We can feel relief by allowing the emotion/energy to move through us, or we can find it through the ease of doing something else, like meditation or a walk.

The energy will loop in on itself and create similar thoughts, feelings, and situations if we don't allow it to move up. Moreover, the more we think these thoughts, the easier it will become to think them the next time. We need to find ease about our emotions whenever we can to begin the process of slowing down the momentum in this environment.

We all feel the relief of blame; we all try to take our power back through anger. We all feel the same emotions.

It's okay to be here if here is where you find yourself. It's only a small jump up into a better-feeling environment. A small shift in energy is all it takes. You can do that.

What it Attracts:

If there's an area in our lives where we blame someone for doing something that made us angry, then that will also affect the other areas of our lives. Every time we think about that person and feel that anger and blame again, we reenergize this environment. And we feel that on all levels.

If we keep talking about it, if we keep telling the same story of anger and blame, we will keep feeding the energy. This will not only keep that subject in this environment, but it will also soon start pulling other subjects in it, as well. We'll start feeling angry about everything and everyone. Simple remarks will send us over the edge. Simple chores around the house will make us crazy.

This is what happens with dominant energies, also known as frequent feelings. The feeling begins to affect all the other areas of our lives, as well. It then becomes a home environment, where most of our issues live. We constantly find ourselves feeling this way. Everything we do, everything others say, brings us right back to these feelings.

As we're angry about one subject, someone else might approach us with another and trigger our anger. We're now suddenly angry about a subject that was fine yesterday. We've now pulled that into this environment, as well. It's easy to stay angry once we're angry. It's easy to keep the momentum going.

We will keep attracting people and events that remind us of the same feeling. It will get triggered over and over again throughout the day, each day. More people will make us angry. More issues will be pulled here. It will begin to spread all over our lives. We will feel the need to blame others for it. We might even blame one person for everything. If we look at our lives as a chain of reactions, we might bring it back to one event and one person. We might become even more angry and bitter, hating that person for ruining our lives. We might not be able to enjoy anything else.

It's easy to fall into this emotional cycle and drag other topics into it because emotions can be like a tornado. It will pull in anything that is nearby. As we direct more attention and energy to it, it will grow bigger and bigger, taking more and more.

Blame leads to more events that feel out of our control. Anger leads to more events that make us angry. It will take in more issues, more people around us, and more experiences. New experiences will change to match the energy and emotion of it; even old experiences will feel different now. All emotions feed on themselves if they are not eased or allowed to move up naturally, so it will just compound with each new experience.

Soon, we'll get to a place where people can't even say hello to us or ask a simple question without triggering our anger. The world will feel heavy, hard, and burdensome. Everything will feel like a struggle, a battle, a fight.

The more we practice these emotions, the more we stay here and create from here, the easier it is to come here. The emotional pathways we create will have more ease each time we use them. Jumping from anger to rage might become easier and easier each time we do it because we're building momentum in that direction. We are linking them in our emotional experiences. In the same way, jumping from anger to ease can become so easy that we might not even feel the need to become angry long. We will learn to just go straight to ease after a few minutes of anger.

As we create or change these pathways, we will change the speed and ease in which we attract people and experiences. We might be feeling hopeful dominantly, but then have a moment of anger. That won't change our attraction because hopefulness is our dominant energy. We mainly pull in experiences from there, so a few moments of anger won't change anything. As soon as we find ease, we'll be back in our home environment of hope.

However, if we're dominantly angry and we feel a little bit of ease, we will immediately feel and see the difference in our attraction. Going from negative emotion into a relieving one will always show us the difference in the type of feedback we receive from others and from life. However, going from positive to negative will only be felt first, but it won't necessarily show up in our lives immediately. It might take some time.

Positive feeling momentum moves energy very powerfully. Negative energy doesn't really exist. There is only positive energy and the resistance of positive energy. The "negative" emotions are simply the act of introducing resistance to positive energy and slowing it down, depression being the slowest-moving energy. It's like applying the brakes to slow down the car. There is no negative acceleration pedal that will take us down a negative road. There is only one acceleration pedal and one brake pedal to slow down the energy. We always get to steer. We are in control of how fast we go and where we go.

This is a good thing. It means that a little bit of ease goes a long way in allowing the energy to flow again. All we have to do is just take our foot off the (resistance) brake and let it speed up. It takes a lot of practiced resistance to slow it down and just a bit of ease to speed it up.

This means that using the brakes doesn't stop us immediately — it just slows down the positive energy a bit. This is why we don't immediately see negative experiences once we have negative emotions. We didn't stop anything; we just slowed it down for a bit. We would have to have a lot of negative emotion practiced for a while before it begins to affect our physical lives.

Speeding up is something we can feel and experience immediately. Going 5 miles per hour to 20 miles per hour is a big difference and can be felt immediately. We are getting there faster, we are moving faster. It feels better. It feels easier. Things become easier.

Sometimes, when we're moving too fast, when we get too happy, we introduce some resistance to slow it down. We hit the brakes because the speed at which we're moving scares us. So we create problems just to slow down the energy.

We might begin to have doubts or suspect unusual things. We might pick fights or become needy. We might cause drama or even cheat. We might tell off our bosses or do something without thinking. We might fail on purpose or lie. We might ruin our relationships or opportunities because the speed scared us. It happens often.

Then, we might come down into this environment where we feel angry with others or ourselves. We might blame them for what we did. We might blame them for making us too happy and scaring us into hitting the brakes. We might even feel angry with ourselves for believing we could ever be happy. Maybe we're just used to this speed.

We can always speed back up any time we choose. Hitting the brakes doesn't mean the end of anything. Energy doesn't end. It can be redirected somewhere else, and it can be slowed, but it won't stop. It can't.

What we attract from anger and blame can be shifted immediately through some ease and relaxation. We can start moving again. We can be happy again. All we need is a bit of ease. That's all it takes to get us rolling again.

Thought Clusters:

This environment is likely to compound a certain cluster of thoughts. One thought will trigger another like it, and that will trigger the next. We can spend minutes or hours thinking these types of thoughts, which feeds the energy of the environment. We rarely ever just think one of these thoughts — that's why they're called clusters. They usually pull each other into the thought process and are never isolated.

Thought clusters in projection can be exactly or similar to the following:

"He did this to me!"
"I'm so stupid!"
"It's all my fault!"
"She's so stupid!"
"It's all her fault!"
"Why can't I be beautiful like her?"
"My life would be better if I were rich like him."
"I want to feel powerful, too."
"It's your fault I'm angry!"
"You're always doing this to me!"

Thoughts in projection tend to focus mostly on others. Our faults are others' faults. What we hate about ourselves, we direct toward others in anger. We blame everything in our lives on them. We project our feelings onto them so we don't have to deal with it.

If we fall into the cycle of thought --> emotion --> more similar thoughts --> more similar emotions, we become people who are just generally angry. Nothing will please us or make us feel better. We will begin to look for relief in more aggressive or violent ways. Our thoughts, feelings, and words will turn into actions against others.

Nothing in the lower environments feels more powerful than righteous anger. Feelings that are justified are more likely to be fed with more justifiable thoughts until they become justifiable actions.

There must be an interruption in the cycle of thinking and feeling, a change in focus from the negative to the positive. We will either have to consciously ease into another emotion or trigger one.

What To Do:

The first five environments will often loop on each other and can do so all within a few minutes. You want to interrupt the looping process through relief or distraction. Anger can lead to blame, which can lead to rage, which can lead to shame, which can lead to depression, which can lead to disappointment, which can lead to pessimism, which can lead to depression again, which can lead to hate. All of this can happen within one conversation. If you can, get off of the topic or step away from the conversation.

The first course of action in any of the first five lower environments is to find relief. You can find relief through body mindfulness or distraction. You can feel the feeling and allow it to dissipate, or you can pick up a book, go for a walk, or watch a comedy.

You can explore your thoughts and emotions to find the reason for your reactions, but it's best to do that from higher environments. If you attempt that from here, you'll only feel more blame and anger. The thoughts will loop. You'll dig deeper in this environment. It's important to self-reflect, learn, and grow — it's just very difficult to do it from here.

If we can't seem to find relief through distraction, then we can move up into the next closest environment. Anger, blame, and jealousy almost always lead to feeling disappointed. This is a natural step up. As long as we don't judge our disappointment into depression or shame ourselves back down to victimhood, we are on the right track.

If you feel angry about something, then something most likely happened in a way you did not want, choose, or expect. Some people say, "You should feel angry about this!" Yes, by all means, feel the anger, but also remember that there is a feeling of disappointment and hurt underneath the anger.

Start feeling disappointed about what happened. You're welcome to feel doubt about how well it could possibly end. Feel free to be negative about the outcome.

If you choose, you can take out a pen and paper and write down all the things about the situation that you feel disappointed or upset about. Ask yourself, is there something you can do about this aspect? How about this one? If there is, put a star next to it, if there isn't, cross it off; that one is out of your control for now.

Feel what you need to feel around the parts you can't control. Feel angry, feel disappointed, or blame someone.

All emotions must be allowed. Nothing should be resisted because resistance feeds cycles. Allow the anger, then allow disappointment, and allow the pessimism. When you allow it, it has a shorter lifespan. The more you resist and judge your emotions, the longer you stretch out the process of relieving them.

If you feel resistance toward allowing an emotion, accept your resistance. Acknowledge it, and allow it. "I accept my resistance toward my anger." "I accept my refusal to fully feel my anger." "I allow my resistance." Allowing yourself to refuse something can bring you relief. You can't force yourself either way. Something must be accepted, even if you're accepting your refusal to accept something else.

If you need to take some time to feel the disappointment of how things occurred, you're welcome to take it. It would be best to find ease in your emotions by letting them happen as they are happening.

There's nothing wrong with anger. If you're upset because things didn't happen the way you wanted them to, it's okay to feel angry or disappointed. That's very natural. It's okay to be angry that you're sick. It's okay to feel angry that your husband left you.

More than that, it's perfectly okay to feel disappointed that you became sick or that your husband left you. It's okay to be disappointed that you didn't get the grades you wanted or the car you dreamed of.

Whenever you feel angry about something, there is an underlying disappointment that wants to be felt. But first, you have to feel the anger. The anger won't allow you to move into disappointment until you have allowed it to finish out its natural process.

It's the same with the emotion of blame, except it's much easier to be disappointed from blame than from anger. If you can move your anger into blame, then you can easily move it into disappointment.

Jealousy is a much easier emotion to move into disappointment because it's softer than the other two. When you are jealous of someone, you are feeling some level of disappointment that you do not have what they have.

The fastest way to move up from jealousy is to allow the feeling of disappointment or doubt. It's okay to think you will never have what they have. That's pessimism, and it's a natural climb up. As long as you don't dip yourself back into depression or shame, you will easily move up from there.

You can move through the first five environments in your mind very quickly. 1. Depression: I hate my life. 2. Shame: I'm always screwing it up. 3. Rage: I can't do anything right! 4. Blame: Everything is my fault! 4. Jealousy: I wish I were like my sister. She has her life figured out. 5. Pessimism: I'll never figure out my life.

Your emotions are always naturally moving up. In one paragraph of self-talk we moved through five environments. Let it happen. Allow them to go through their process. Just keep reaching for the thoughts that bring relief. Try to find ease with them. You're not a bad person for thinking or feeling anything.

You are a human being with a large scale of emotions that you are capable of feeling. In your life, you will feel all of them — some more than others. All of that will depend on energetic momentum and your own judgment system.

The less you judge yourself for your emotions, the easier this whole process will become. Take it easy. We all feel everything you're feeling. You're not alone in your emotions.

We've all felt depressed, we've all been angry with ourselves, we've all blamed someone or something for our lives, we've all had doubts, we've all hated some aspect of ourselves; nothing you are going through is a completely unique emotional experience. Nothing. Even if the situation feels unique, the emotions around it aren't. They can't be. If one human being can feel it, we all can feel it.

Do you feel that relief? Take a breath. Let's move up.

Environment 5:
The Pessimists
Doubt, Disappointment, Skepticism

The Energy of The Pessimists:

Skepticism can feel like an emotionally safe place. Mostly because we talk ourselves out of actions and beliefs that feel risky. There isn't much allowance of desire in this environment because there is a fear of disappointment. It feels better to not believe in something positive or have hope in a better outcome than to feel disappointed and let down.

If something didn't work out the way we expected, we might dip down into depression, anger, or blame, and that possibility can frighten us and stop us from allowing ourselves to truly want something that doesn't feel safe or like a guarantee. We might choose to be pessimistic as a form of protection from more negative emotions that don't feel good.

However, disappointment and pessimism are in the same environment. We don't change the environment when we become pessimistic to avoid disappointments. We only change our perception of whether we have control over our experiences.

When we are disappointed, it feels as though other people or circumstances have control over what happens to us. When we are skeptics or pessimists, we feel more powerful when people let us down or disappoint us because we were expecting it. We feel more powerful when we declare, "That's not gonna happen," as opposed to, "I wanted it to happen, but it didn't."

The result, however, is the same; we are still in this environment. Progress in pessimism is not allowed. It's suspect. We approach it with caution, with negative expectation. We don't trust any of it.

What we don't realize is that the energy and expectation for disappointment can be more powerful than our desire for a better outcome. Our pessimism might not allow us to truly enjoy opportunities or events because we're expecting something negative to ruin it. We may *want* a better life, but if we're pessimistic about it due to past disappointments then we're less likely to take risks, trust new people, or embrace new opportunities.

When we drop to this environment after we hoped for a desired outcome, it hurts. The higher up we were, the more painful it is to fall into this environment. It's less painful to stay here.

It feels much safer to stay in an emotional environment of no positive expectation or desire. If there is no drop, we don't feel the pain. We get to be right about our experiences, even if they are limited.

So many of us choose not to dare to hope because it's safer here. We choose to stay in pessimism, not understanding that we are in the same emotional environment as the disappointment from which we're running.

That's why when we act from this environment, we almost always end up disappointed: because the energy feeds itself. The energy started in this environment, and so it brings it back to this environment.

If we begin in pessimism, we can stay here for a long time without feeling disappointment or other negative emotions. We just get to be right about other people letting us down. We get our disappointed feeling confirmed and validated. We continue to deny hope, and so we rarely dip back down into the lower environments, and that feels okay. Most people call it being realistic. But what is realism other than receiving what we expect?

We can expect success, love, kindness from others, or we can expect others to let us down, hate us, judge us, etc. We can expect from better environments.

We mostly expect through the type of questions we ask ourselves on a daily basis. The majority of the thinking process is asking and answering questions within our own minds. Even when it doesn't seem like we're asking a question, there is an underlining one we don't recognize.

We might think, "I hate my body" is a statement and not a question, but it is most likely a thought that came after a question like, "Why don't I look good in this?" Or, "Why do I feel so horrible? Am I fat? Can I lose weight? Why can't I look like her?"

We don't realize that we ask ourselves questions every day about everything. The quality of our questions determines our experiences as either positive or negative. There are questions that elicit optimistic expectations, and there are questions that elicit pessimistic expectations. In other words, we ask the questions with an expectation already in place for the answer. We set ourselves up for positive or negative responses. We are realistic in either case because both create our very real experiences.

If we feel horrible about our bodies and then ask the question, "Am I fat?" we are not going to answer positively or optimistically. In that state, we are likely to ask questions that continue to make us feel worse. We feel bad and we expect to continue to feel bad, and so we ask ourselves questions that perpetuate that feeling.

We are constantly asking ourselves questions about ourselves, about the people around us, and about our lives. They feed how we feel and keep the energy going.

If we woke up in the morning and asked, "What am I going to do today?" we will get a very different emotional response from, "What can I do today that I would enjoy?" or, "How can I have some fun today?"

Can you feel the difference between, "Why did this happen to me?" verses "How can I solve this?" "How can I progress in this situation?" "What's within my power?"

The mind wants to automatically answer all the questions that are posed to it. As pessimists, we always set up questions that support limitation or disbelief. We then begin expecting those experiences of limitations.

It's important to ask the questions that lead to an empowering conclusion. We don't want to ask questions that depress us, upset us, or make us feel more pessimistic.

We want to ask the questions that leave us open to more possibilities. If we ask questions that push us into corners, we'll feel limited in our answers.

Even if we don't immediately answer the questions, we can feel the difference in them. As pessimists and optimists, we would ask ourselves very different questions within the same situation.

As pessimists, we would wonder what we were going to lose. Who is cheating us? What kind of damage are we going to sustain? Who is trying to take advantage of us?

As optimists, we might wonder how we can create an outcome where both parties win. What would be the best course of action? What can I do with what I know now? Who would be the best person to get advice from in this situation? How can we resolve this fairly?

If we can become more conscious of what we ask ourselves, we can change our feelings about any situation.

"Why did this happen to me?" feels very different from "What can I learn from this?" If we bombard ourselves with pessimistic questions that lead to pessimistic answers, then we'll eventually depress ourselves by losing hope.

Most of our interactions with others are about answering the questions we have in our minds. We are almost always responding to our own questions.

When we ask someone else a question, there is another deeper question we are really trying to answer for ourselves. We don't flat out ask, "Can I trust you?" Instead, we ask, "So why did you and your last girlfriend break up?"

In this case, we're not really listening to their answer; we're listening for OUR answer. We're trying to find the answer to our own underlining questions. "Is he trustworthy? What is he saying about her? Will he say the same about me? Will he leave me, too?" He may not realize it, but he's really answering those questions.

We do this every day. We ask questions, and then we evaluate the answers so we can judge how we should respond. Just look at children. They can ask hundreds of questions in a day because they're learning to evaluate information so they know how to respond to life.

As pessimists, we're usually looking for what's wrong, and we find it because the mind doesn't do gaps in knowledge. It will find a way to fill it in, either with truth or fiction.

Since the mind always finds the answers it seeks, it finds the negatives because that's really what we're seeking. Maybe we're looking for an excuse or reason to not do something or to give up. Maybe we're looking for an excuse not to trust someone. And if we only focus on the negativities, we can talk ourselves out of everything. This might make us feel safe. It's safer to assume someone is going to betray you than to take the risk and trust them.

We ask the questions that expose negativities because there is a sense of comfort in knowing them. There are no surprises and therefore no uncertainty, which is what really scares us.

There is an underlying feeling of fear, anxiety, or worry behind the questions, but not enough to place us in Environment 2. There's a sense of control over them in this environment, and that gives us a sense of comfort. We feel some control in our worry.

However, we don't have to fear negative emotion or dips in emotions. Once we learn how to consciously move up, once we create momentum in finding ease and relief, we can easily do so from disappointment. We don't have to avoid emotion and play it safe. We don't have to worry to feel in control.

Emotion is not our enemy. It only feels like a scary thing because we don't understand its processes. We haven't learned how to consciously allow its movement. We haven't learned enough ease. We don't trust ourselves yet. We have self-doubt. This makes us want to skip the emotional journey and end up where we think we're headed anyway.

However, there is no such thing as a permanent emotion. We skip, jump, and dip in and out of emotions daily. We journey into them and this journey is not a straight line with a permanent destination.

If we were setting out on a vacation to a beautiful island and we didn't know what was waiting for us there, would we cancel the trip? We could end up with a few days of relaxation and fun, or rain and problems. We don't know for sure. We don't know what awaits us. Do we take the risk anyway? Most do.

So imagine if we just decide, "Well I'm gonna end up coming back home anyway, so why go? I could just skip the journey and go straight to the destination." But we don't go on vacation because we want to end up at home where it's safe. We risk our sense of safety for the possibilities of fun, exploration, relaxation, and adventure.

All emotions are internal experiences. Some can feel like relaxing vacations, and others can feel like hell. They all help us in the long run either way. They help us figure out what we really want. They help focus us in the direction we would rather go.

Every unwanted experience is simply clarification for a wanted one. We don't have to cycle through lower environments for years and years. If we learn how to allow the natural movement up, we can breeze through the environments we don't want to be in and build more momentum in the environments we do want.

We don't have to play it safe with our emotions because we are in control of them. There is no safe environment because they're all safe. They're all within our energetic control. We can shift them immediately through relief.

How do most people avoid feeling worry and anxiety? They don't allow themselves to believe that anything good will ever happen. That way, if it does, they're pleasantly surprised. They get to be practical and realistic, and if something nice happens, then they get joy. It feels safe. However, the less we expect, the less we receive, which just validates the feelings of limitation and skepticism.

Or, we can do it the natural way and find ease in higher environments where worry doesn't even exist. There is no worry in joy or in passion and eagerness. This is why some of the most successful people dare the most—because to them, they're not daring. Courage to them doesn't feel like courage. It feels like ease. Passion is guiding them. Not worry. Not playing it safe. Not skepticism.

Have you heard of regular everyday people running into burning buildings and saving others without a second thought? We call them heroes because we admire their courage. They don't feel courageous at all because they weren't afraid in the first place. It came easily to them. They were inspired by the moment, and they acted on it. Risk and loss didn't enter their minds. Courage is only courage when we have to fight through fear to act.

That's how powerful emotions are. We can take the hardest task, the bravest task, and accomplish them easily by being in the right emotional space. By allowing the energy to carry us instead of forcing the energy to align, which is impossible.

If we choose the common way to avoid anxiety, by worrying, as many do, that leaves our feelings and life to chance. Maybe something good will happen and surprise us while we're being skeptical, maybe it won't and we'll be right about everything. Either way, it feels like a win.

But chance doesn't exist. We create from our emotional environments, and so being "practical" or limited will only create more of the same.

So you're right. You are always right. You're right about not being able to trust anyone. You're right about people being liars. You're right about it all. The universe only validates our feelings. Why? Because they're personal facts. You WILL get back what you feel. Always. And if you ask the right questions, you can keep yourself feeling validated in any emotion.

That's the thing about emotions; they're always true for you. You're right about everything you feel. You are, in fact, justified in your practicality or skepticism. You are justified in your anger and aggression. You are perfect in your depression. You are right. Don't fight any of it. Accept it as it is, and let it pass so you can be right about better emotions.

What it Attracts:

We are only limited by our beliefs. A pessimistic mindset will only allow circumstances and people who fit into the limits of that thinking. Believing that people always lie will attract liars. Believing that people will betray us will attract betrayals. Believing that there are only two possibilities will show us just that.

We receive and allow within the possibilities of what we believe. Nothing "wild" can happen if we believe it's wild and therefore not within the normal expectance of our lives. This is why we keep cycling through similar experience with different people who *feel* familiar.

We tend to set our limits based on what we have experienced so far. As skeptics, we especially set our limits in a place that feels comfortable and safe, usually limiting it to what we have already experienced.

Anything we want to create has to feel normal for us first. It has to be believable. We can hope for a $100 increase in our monthly income, but $1,000 might feel unrealistic. We're going to be practical about it and only think of the $100. This creates a limiting mindset that won't even allow us to see the opportunities for more. We won't be able to see the avenues for a higher increase because we don't believe it's possible. Not yet anyway. Not from this environment.

Someone might catch us on a good day and make an offer that changes our mind about our current possibilities, but that can only happen if we are in a higher environment in the moment. We either won't get the offer in this environment, we won't believe it, or we won't follow through on it. If it doesn't match, it will fall away somehow.

As skeptics, we are ultimately seeking emotional security. We want certainty in what we're feeling. If we're going to feel hope, we need a guarantee that it will work out. We can't dare to hope unless hope feels practical in the moment.

It's an emotionally better place to be than depression, rage, or anger. There is a much better sense of emotional control here. But if we stop here and settle, we can miss out on a lot of joy, passion, fun, and adventure.

We might also become dream killers for those around us. We can easily take joyful and passionate people with little doubts and introduce more doubts and pessimism into their dreams.

As doubters, we can easily magnify the doubts in others. Just like how an angry person can easily anger someone else who is emotionally close by.

If we build a lot of momentum in this environment, we can become unpleasant to everyone we love because we just negate everything they say or do. We might not like happy people. In fact, they might annoy us, thus moving us up into the next environment.

That is a good step up, provided we don't dip back down, creating a cycle of pessimism and annoyance. Then, we become grumps who are always annoyed at someone about something and can't see any possibility of resolution for anything.

From this environment, we will only attract people who can offer us possibilities within our limitations. Everything else will feel exaggerated or like a waste of time.

If, however, we are to ignore our skepticism and accept something just on the off chance that we might be wrong about our pessimism, we will create an experience that will show us that we were right in the first place.

Energy doesn't do wishy-washy. In other words, emotion can't split and offer you two different outcomes. The most powerful emotion will win each time, and that will depend mostly on momentum. If our skepticism is stronger than our hope that it could turn out differently this time, then we will be disappointed.

There is more momentum in this environment, and so it prevails. Our desire for hope must be stronger than the "evidence" we see around us. This is what faith is, which is the opposite of doubt.

The circumstances and people we attract into our lives are based on our mindsets. If we try to prove it wrong, we will only fortify it.

Skepticism and pessimism are very limiting mindsets that can keep us cycling through similar experiences for years. And the more we try to fight our way out of it, the more it will validate itself in our experience. All emotions are like that. The more we fight them, the more they win.

We can't stand in an environment and then try to disprove it. That doesn't work because the environment always feeds and reinforces itself. We always get the evidence of it in our experience. We must move up and let the environment, along with everything in it, naturally shift.

Thought Clusters:

This environment is likely to compound a certain cluster of thoughts. One thought will trigger another like it, and that will trigger the next. We can spend minutes or hours thinking these types of thoughts, which feeds the energy of the environment. We rarely ever just think one of these thoughts — that's why they're called clusters. They usually pull each other into the thought process and are never isolated.

Thought clusters in skepticism can be exactly or similar to the following:

"Yeah, right. That's never going to happen."
"Don't waste your time."

"I don't believe that."
"You can't trust anyone."
"People are liars."
"Everyone will betray you. "
"I highly doubt that."
"Nothing is going to work out."
"People don't want to see you happy."
"This is my life now. It's not going to change."

Thoughts in pessimism tend to be doubtful in nature. This is the environment opposite of hope and faith, so it is the environment of limited expectation.

The thoughts, the questions, and the answers all match the expectation of the environment. Since the environment tends to be pessimistic in nature, we receive responses that reinforce it more.

Very little seems possible in this environment. The thoughts produced here are created to make the thinker feel safe. It becomes a comfort zone.

There must be an interruption in the cycle of thinking and feeling or else we will be stuck living the same day for years and years. We will either have to consciously ease into another emotion or trigger one.

What To Do:

Changing the questions you ask yourself can be a very effective method of finding ease and relief. First ask, can I do something to change this situation? What can I do? How do I feel about this? How do I want to feel? Is there something I can do now to begin changing how I feel? Is there a better outcome?

Create a set of questions when you're in a better mood and look at them when you are faced with an issue. Allow your mind to find better solutions. Sit with each question for a few minutes and see what comes up.

If it's too negative or makes you angry, then step away from it for a little while, distract yourself with something else, and then come back to the questions. If you can take a few deep breaths and maybe do a calming meditation for two minutes, you'll feel the difference in your answers to those questions.

If there is a problem, there is a solution. If there is a negative way to look at something, there is a positive way. If a situation can feel hopeless, then it can feel hopeful. There are multiple possibilities in all situations. We only see what we expect, and if we're used to not expecting much, then that is what we will get.

If you find yourself in a pessimistic environment frequently, you have most likely chosen it as a safe home environment that won't let you dip or rise often. This environment is cautious of hope because it has often led to disappointment.

One of the most effective things you can do in this environment is to take away the fear of disappointment. There is far too much power placed on this emotion. It creates a need for avoidance, which keeps you pessimistic.

So what if something doesn't work out the way you want it to? How many people get exactly what they want, when they want it, and in the way they want it every single time? No one.

Is there another way? Is there something else that can be done? Can you accept that there is more than just one path or possibility for a positive outcome?

Life is a continuous growing experience, and we don't grow until we experience. Disappointment is not the end of the line. It's simply a request for more clarification on what we want. "Okay, so I liked that aspect, but I didn't like that one." Good! Now, you know what you don't like or what you don't want! Fantastic. You have more experience now. You've now grown. You'll make different choices next time.

If you don't ruminate in the emotion and use it as an excuse to dip down into lower environments, then you can attract something that is even better than what you initially wanted because now, you have more clarity.

The first time around, you noticed that you liked 20% of what happened and didn't like the other 80%. Great! More clarity for you! So you try something different with your newfound clarity, and this time you like 40% and don't like 60%. Fantastic! More progress!

The third time might be 50/50 or even better. But if you're always focusing on what disappoints you rather than noticing where you're improving, you'll never feel like you're making any progress. You'll eventually depress yourself and you won't try again. Pessimists tend to give up after the first try.

Have you really not learned anything from your "negative" experiences? Of course you have. Human beings are learning machines; it's impossible not to learn something. You just have to learn to give yourself credit for it. Instead of expecting less the next time just to avoid disappointment, refocus your attention on your progress. How is this situation different? Can you see how you did things differently this time? Can we feel that something has changed?

From this environment, you can jump right into hope if you find ways to ease yourself with your thoughts. Ask the right questions to change your focus, and you'll be right there with each answer. If you are disappointed by

20% of the situation, focus on the 80% you liked. Regardless of how small the number is, focus on what you liked, and you will multiply that in your experience.

Focus on the thought that feels better. Something negative happened, and you didn't like the outcome. Feeling disappointed about it is much better than feeling like you deserved it or telling yourself you can't be happy. Don't make your disappointment wrong, but don't place too much weight on in either. It doesn't mean anything.

You expected something to be one way, and it turned out another. That's life. If you begin to see better, you will begin to feel better; when you feel better, you continue to see better. On and on it cycles. You are much more likely to make progress and see better results from a positive environment than from a negative one.

It won't matter how much you're trying or advancing if you're feeling negative. You will eventually find a way to discourage yourself and feel like it's all just a waste of time. This is also true the other way around.

It's not a hard jump to make if you have some momentum going in that environment. If you have ever felt some hope, you have some momentum there. And if you find yourself in this environment, then you have certainly felt some hope because hope and doubt are two sides of the same coin.

If you can find some ease in this environment, you can easily flip the coin over to hope. It's a much quicker jump from here and can happen within a few seconds. Ask yourself the right question, and you will feel the relief long before you can come up with an answer. Just knowing it's possible is enough. That's hope.

Just knowing there is hope, that it's not all doom and gloom, is enough. Just knowing that there is a possibility that something can work out is enough. In this environment, we don't need miracles or big strides. We don't even believe in them. We just need a little bit of change.

Have some fun, hope a little, and take it easy. Do something you like. Do something you don't like, and see if you like it now. Try something new. Be easy with yourself. Dare to hope. Dare to love. Dare to live. Take a risk.

Disappointment doesn't have to mean anything if you don't take it personally and make it about your worthiness. It has nothing to do with who you are. We all feel it.

It's an emotion that can easily be shifted. Feel the relief of that statement. Disappointment is not a big deal. It's an emotion, and you have plenty of those. All kinds of emotions! Disappointment is just one of many. It helps us clarify our desires. When we learn about what we don't want, we can focus on what we do want. No need to marinate over what we didn't like. No need to hang onto that. There are so many others to choose from.

If you can focus on the other aspects of your life that feel better, you can ease the feeling of disappointment. Or you can allow yourself to get frustrated and annoyed. That works, too!

It's ultimately your choice which route you want to take. If annoyance feels better, then go down that road. If you can't find a little bit of hope or relief, get annoyed.

Environment 6:
The Annoyed
Frustration, Irritation, Overwhelmed

The Energy of The Annoyed:

In this environment, everything that once felt normal can become annoying. Someone chewing, speaking, or sitting in a particular way can annoy us. A dog barking in the distance, a fly buzzing around, a child playing nearby; anything that might have gone unnoticed in any other environment will be noticed in this one.

When we are annoyed, we tend to be the grumps. We have very little patience for anyone and can have quick comebacks to other people's responses. We are annoyed by others and usually end up annoying others with our annoyances.

We can get annoyed with people who are depressed, people who are suffering, people who are just sitting and not doing anything else, even people who are happy, maybe they're too happy, and that bothers us. Nothing pleases us when we are annoyed. We might even begin to annoy ourselves.

This comes from a place of frustration. It tends to be general in nature, and that's why it's higher on the levels. Energetically, it's softer to be annoyed than angry.

Frustration is the softest of the aggressive energies. Rage being the strongest one. It is much easier to calm frustration than rage. It's also a much shorter jump into hope from here.

Frustration is usually a symptom of force or control. We want something to work out, but it's not going according to our vision or idea. Maybe someone said something we didn't want to hear. Perhaps they acted in a way we weren't expecting or didn't like. Perhaps we feel impatient because we want things to move faster.

We want something to change or be different, and there's some form of control or force we're trying to use to change it. This creates resistance, which slows down things even more.

We can't use force and control to make things work more easily because those are in resistance, and resistance is what dips us down into lower environments, where there is little ease. Force can't create ease. The more resistance we add, the lower we dip, and the less ease we have. Frustration can then turn into rage, which can turn into shame, and then hopelessness.

When we are in lower environments, we don't easily attract good-feeling events or situations. They don't feel smooth in their appearance or execution and can cause us more frustration.

Trying to control, force, or manipulate anything adds more resistance into whichever environment we are in, which keeps us frustrated and feeling more out of control. The more we feel out of control, the harder we fight to keep control. Once again, the energy feeds itself.

It's easier to dip down into pessimism from this environment because we can become tired of fighting for control and just resign into skepticism about anything working in our favor. We can't see ease. We can't feel ease, and so we become pessimistic about it happening in our lives.

When we are frustrated, we believe that we have to fight for everything and that nothing comes easily. We also tend to be skeptics about most things, especially ease.

It becomes a faraway dream, something that only happens to other people. Maybe rich people, or lucky people, but no one "normal." Everyone else has to fight and work hard for what they want. And so we live in a state of readiness to struggle.

We might fight with the lamp that won't turn on, or we might fight with our co-worker who doesn't understand what we're saying. We might fight with a child who won't listen, or a partner who couldn't read our minds and take out the garbage. We might fight with our computers or phones. We are always ready for the next battle for control.

We live in a state of frustration because we want to be powerful and create changes in our lives. However, we have a misguided definition of power, and so it keeps us locked in frustration. We think it's the ability to control other people and things through force. However, that doesn't give us power — that only creates a bigger frustrated power struggle.

The only power we have or need is the power over our emotions. That is all we ever need to control. If we want better relationships, if we want better jobs, or people to be nicer to us, to respect us, then all we have to do is focus on our emotions. When we change the environment we are in, we will change everything around us easily and without struggle, hard work, or force. It will happen naturally.

No one likes to be around someone who is trying to control or manipulate them. They can feel the forcefulness in our energy. That doesn't make them want to work with us, date us, comply with us, or even be around us.

When we are more easy-going and light, doors will open for us more easily. People will bring us more opportunities for success because they will like our energy. There will be "something about you" that they won't be able to pinpoint. Something that makes them want you to have the good opportunities. Something that makes them want to push for your promotion. Something that makes them become fans of you, and they won't even understand why. That's how powerful energy is. It can bring the right people to your side and open doors where you once saw walls.

If you had an opening for a position in your workplace, would you give it to the person who was friendly, fun, easy-going and a people person, or would you give it to the frustrated grump who was always trying to control the people around him to make himself feel better?

People don't want to work with that energy. They don't want to give good opportunities to people who are always fighting or negative. They want to give the opportunities to people who match it with their energy, people who "deserve" it, which is really another word for a match.

The only power we have is over our emotions. That may not seem like a lot, but it's everything. It's everything that has been creating our world up to this point. If we want to create better lives, we have to become more conscious of our thoughts and emotions.

When we learn how to consciously ease ourselves, we will find everything falling into place. People we don't want to work with will suddenly get transferred. Our noisy neighbors will get evicted. Friends who were negative won't want to talk to us anymore. People will drop out of our lives, and new people will come in. Things will begin to shift around. Not because we were fighting to control those things, but because we learned how to control the only thing we have any control over, which is our emotions. All we have to do is change the environment and let everything that doesn't match it simply fall away.

What it Attracts:

Every environment attracts to it more of the same. Frustration, which is dependent on our need for control, can create events that feel out of our control, which only makes us more frustrated.

The most common occurrence in this environment is an accident of some kind. However, an accident might not make everyone feel out of control, so it will depend on each person's thoughts and feelings about the event. No one feeling attracts a specific event. It all depends on what the event elicits in each person. Usually, accidents do make people feel out of control and frustrated. So we might fall, break something, accidently hit something, or create some kind of event that feels random and not asked for.

Pain can also make us feel out of control, which is why we often attract what feels like random pain, like stubbing our toe or hitting our arm. We are not intentionally hurting ourselves, so the fact that it creates more frustration within us is a signal that we're feeling out of control in some area. Something is not going according to plan. These accidents tend to be little indicators of where we are in our emotions and energy.

It's the perfect opportunity to find ease wherever we can. If we don't, we might wake up stubbing our toe and then create a chain of events that keep us annoyed and frustrated all day.

You've heard these stories before and maybe even lived them yourself. First, you wake up, and then some little thing happens as an indication of where you are energetically, but instead of paying attention and consciously shifting, you just become frustrated.

Then, another thing occurs, and then another. You can't find your keys, and you're running late. Your car is making noises. Great, now you have to schedule an appointment to get it checked out—another hassle. You arrive late to work only to be hassled some more, which is the last thing you need. Your important client cancels on you. At that moment, you get a text from your partner that says they're mad at you for something you did. Suddenly, it feels like a "bad" day.

How can you "control" any of these events? For most of us, we yell, fight, and push back to feel a sense of control. We think we have to do something about what's in front of us just because it's in front of us. However, what's in front of us is only a mirror of what's happening inside of us. We can't fight the mirror for what it's showing us.

The power we have is in our responses. The power we have is in our emotions going forward. Even if we may have missed the first ten signs, we can still turn it around on the eleventh.

If we were to take a few minutes in the morning to ease the initial incident, we would be able to divert all the other events away from us. Even when we think we don't have the time for it, we still have to make the time because if we don't, our whole day will be filled with delays and problems. A few minutes of delay for intentional ease is worth it when the other option is ten hours of frustrations and stress.

If we have time to be grumpy, we have time to find ease. If we have time to be delayed and frustrated, we have time to do short exercises to ease ourselves.

The more we try to avoid running late because we don't want to be frustrated, the more we will create incidents that keep us late and frustrated. There is no avoidance in attraction. We create what we don't want, what we fear, what we want to avoid because it's in the energy of our actions.

We behave in a particular way or commit a specific action because we don't want that thing. However, the energy behind the action is still the thing we don't want. Energy doesn't understand "don't" want. All it understands is "want" and "that thing." There is no don't. There is no avoidance of that thing. Just that thing.

Every time we make a statement in our mind that involves a negative like "don't," all we have to do is just remove the don't and see what we are really asking for. "I don't want to be late." What are we really requesting with our energy? "I want to be late."

We can't "don't" our energy. It doesn't make any sense because energy is about focus, and we can't focus on what we don't want and not pull it into our experience.

Energy flows where it is directed. It can't NOT flow where we don't want it to go when we're paying attention to it. If we direct it onto a fear, that's where it will go. If we pay attention to how frustrated we are and how much things aren't working out in our favor, that's what we will get more of. Energy feeds itself, and it can't feed don't.

Can you not do more of something? Don't think about the fact that you're going to be late and cranky in the morning if you don't get some sleep. Don't think about how your boss is going to find another excuse to reprimand you. Don't think about what a crappy day you're going to have. Don't. Oh, and don't think about how you're going to have a hard time picking out an outfit that fits in the morning. Don't think about how much time you waste doing that. Don't even think about traffic. How do you feel about your day? You should be feeling fine because you said don't think about it, and you didn't. Right?

Just reading those sentences has triggered something in your energy. Even though you are reading a negative, "don't," it is still causing the same feelings. Maybe it made you think about how annoying all of that is. Maybe you thought about how much you hate it or how much you don't want any of it. Just by placing your attention on it and having an emotion about it, you will pull it into your experience. Even if you were thinking "don't."

Don't read this sentence. Why did you read it? I told you not to. Stop reading. But to stop reading, you would have to read it first. You can't *don't* with your energy because you can't *don't* with your attention. You still have to think about it to decide you no longer want to think about it. So how do you stop thinking about it? You think about something else. You don't stop the emotion; you shift it to something else. You replace it.

Attention is what directs the energy so you have to shift your attention to what you want. The more focused you become, the stronger the energy becomes. The energy ends up feeding itself. So if you're practicing the energy as you're thinking you don't want it, you're doing the exact opposite: you're feeding it.

Focus on what you do want instead of trying to avoid what you don't want. This will bring you more ease and less frustration. Every cautious action you take from here will bring you more of the same frustration and delays. Of course, your actions will bring some results. But if the energy isn't right, the actions will tire you or frustrate you. You will feel drained and exhausted and want to quit. It will take you longer to reach your desire, if you reach it. It's easier to relax, find some ease, and then act.

You can reach your desires and goals. You just can't do it by saying the opposite of what you're feeling. You can't trick energy with words; you have to shift it.

Thought Clusters:

This environment is likely to compound a certain cluster of thoughts. One thought will trigger another like it, and that will trigger the next. We can spend minutes or hours thinking these types of thoughts, which feeds the energy of the environment. We rarely ever just think one of these thoughts—that's why they're called clusters. They usually pull each other into the thought process and are never isolated.

Thought clusters in annoyance can be exactly or similar to the following:

"Stop talking, and go away."
"You're getting on my nerves."
"I'm so glad I'm not you."
"You're so annoying."
"I can't do this!"
"Why can't anything ever work out?"
"What else can go wrong?"
"Why can't they just listen to me?"
"Just do what I tell you!"
"I can't take this anymore!"

Thoughts in annoyance are mainly focused on more annoyances. There is little relief here without some kind of action. Unfortunately, most action committed from this environment causes more frustration, which can become overwhelming.

We can become annoyed at birds singing or a bottle cap that won't open. We can become annoyed at any little thing around us. That annoyance and frustration just attracts more thoughts and feelings similar to it. It will either lead to a raging fit, or we will have to consciously calm ourselves down.

Frustrating events can lead to a series of frustrating events if we continue to stay frustrated and pay attention to how frustrated we are.

We can easily fall into a cycle of emotion creating thought, which creates more emotion, which creates more thoughts.

There must be an interruption in the cycle of thinking and feeling. We will either have to consciously ease into another emotion or trigger one.

What To Do:

We have to become easier with people if we want to ease our frustrations. We can ask ourselves a few questions in the moment of frustration. What am I trying to control? Who am I trying to control right now? Why do I want to control them/it? What do I really want from them/it? What is the emotion I'm looking for by trying to control them/it? Can I get that emotion without it being dependent on their behavior or compliance?

When you're frustrated or annoyed, there is very little you will care about. You won't think of this book, you won't care about my words. You won't like exercises. You most likely won't care enough to do them even if you remember them.

Your best bet is to take deep breaths and shift your focus off of what is frustrating you. Once you relax the feeling a bit more, then you can look at what is happening from a calmer perspective. Then, you can ask yourself questions about why you are having that reaction.

It's easy to shift frustration if we can shift the way we look at it. If we can see it for what it is, a struggle for control, we can ease it up.

The irony is that we gain more control by letting go of control. The more okay we are in letting go of control over a situation, the more the situation shifts in a favorable way for us.

As we let go, as we relax, we allow the energy to do what we want it do. If we obsess, fight, struggle, or manipulate, we create a lot of resistance in our own energy, which means it can't flow to where it needs to go and do what it needs to do. It can't pull in our desire when it is heavy with our resistance. Then, we will feel overwhelmed.

The best way to release resistance, outside of meditation, is to move the body. You have to either become really still or really active.

If the frustration is strong and you can't imagine sitting still for meditation without annoying yourself, then let your body release the tension and stress through movement.

Dance, run, do some jumping jacks in place, use a hula-hoop, find an aerobics video online and do it, put on some music and jump around. It really doesn't matter what you do, as long as you get physical for at least twenty minutes. Get your heart rate up.

As your heart starts beating fast, your brain releases good-feeling chemicals and hormones. This relieves your tension and stress. It focuses your mind somewhere else and it benefits your body. When you stop and begin to relax, your brain releases calming chemicals.

You won't feel as frustrated or annoyed. After you rest for about ten minutes, consider doing some meditation afterward. Sit quietly somewhere and focus on your breath for a little while. It doesn't have to be long—five to ten minutes is good enough.

Once you're relaxed, you can look at the same situation but this time from a different emotional place. Ask yourself different questions.

Is there another way to go about this? Is there a conversation I can have with this person that can benefit both of us? What do I want from all of this? Is there a possible resolution I'm not seeing?

You can also try to write down your feelings about the situation or the person when you're frustrated, and then come back to it when you're more relaxed and see where you are adding to the problem. How are you being unreasonable? Where are you not listening? What can you improve about what you're doing or how you're approaching this?

Read your frustrations and ask yourself if this were someone else who came to you with these feelings, how would you respond? Would you become defensive, too, or would you be open to listening to them?

We can't always see how threatening we can become to others when we're frustrated. We can easily isolate people and cause them to become defensive and not even realize that they're just responding to our offense.

Was that the best way to approach someone about that matter? Were you open to listening to them, or were you just expecting them to agree with you? Did you care about their side or version, or were you just looking to vindicate yourself? What were your real intentions when you approached them? Was it to find a resolution for everyone involved or just make yourself feel better?

When we're angry, frustrated, or annoyed, we can't ask those questions without it fueling more anger and frustrations. We have to get to a calmer emotional space before we can relook at the issue. In the meantime, step away, take a bath, meditate, listen to relaxing music, or run, dance, and find a punching bag. Either get really still or really active.

When we become overwhelmed, the energy flows faster than our ability to channel it anywhere. It feels as if life is coming at us fast. Our thoughts race, our hearts race, and our energy becomes a hurricane within us, wrecking havoc on our internal state. You will need to slow it down through meditation or another relaxing exercise before you can find the right solutions. Step away from what is overwhelming you.

Physically change your location to change how you feel. Go for a walk or visit a body of water if you can. Sit by a pool, a lake, river, or beach. Listening to water sounds can create immediate ease. If you're unable to do any of that, find water or nature sounds online and play it in your room. Close your eyes and pretend you're there. It will create the same feeling within you.

You can also distract yourself with an outdoor activity like gardening. Spending time in nature can ease your energy and slow down the overwhelming feelings. Consider also picking up an arts and crafts project like knitting, sculpting, or painting. Build something. Hammer something. Make something that didn't exist before. It'll refocus your energy, calm your emotions, and make you feel productive.

Environment 7:
The Idlers
Impatience, Boredom

The Energy of The Idlers:

Environment 7 is the balancing point between free-flowing energy and resistance. This is the middle emotional environment that deals with a very soft kind of resistance. It's so soft that it's almost nonexistent. The energy begins to flow more freely but doesn't have any particular place to go.

This is the environment of unfocused energy. It's flowing, but it doesn't have a direction. It can easily go in any direction in this environment. We can allow boredom to make us frustrated, or we can use that energy to move us into passion and eagerness. We can pursue our joys, or we can become annoyed.

The environments that came before this one were about some form of control, force, or aggression. There is a little bit of that energy here with impatience, but it's not strong enough to create that level of response. Since the resistance is at its lowest here, there is more energy to flow where we direct it. The issue here is that we don't know what we want to do. We don't know where we want to direct it.

If we can find something to focus the energy on, we can easily move up into eagerness or passion. If we can't, we might become impatient or frustrated, which can begin to weigh us down and dip us into lower environments.

The resistance to free-flowing energy in boredom is very different from the resistance to it in rage. There is no denying the powerful resistance in rage. It is so powerful that it overtakes our entire experience.

Any emotion that feels heavy is full of resistance to free-flowing energy. That's ultimately the only "bad" feeling there ever is. It is the resistance that creates the negative feeling. It is negative of free-flowing energy. The more negative it is, the worse we feel. That's why ease feels so good in the lower environments where there is a lot of resistance. It is the letting go of the resistance that helps the energy flow naturally and move us up into better-feeling environments. Ease frees up the energy. The relief is a sign that we are letting go of resistance.

You won't need to find ease in higher environments because you don't want to ease passion or joy. There is no resistance there. You want to feel those emotions. Ease and relief are only needed from this environment down.

If we are bored, it means we have the free-flowing energy but can't focus it anywhere in particular. We can't find an appropriate activity to direct the energy toward, so it creates the feeling of boredom or impatience.

We don't feel the resistance that weighs us down into a strong emotion, and we don't have the direct focus that can raise us higher into passion or eagerness. The energy is there; it's just undirected.

This can lead us to overeat, lull ourselves through watching TV, surf the internet looking for some kind of stimulation, or just jump on the phone and engage in idle gossip because that excitement feels better than feeling bored. We might create some drama for ourselves because we need something to focus on.

We can't ease boredom; we have to find an avenue for the energy. We have to find an activity that is up to the level of the energy we have. If the activity requires less energy than we have in the moment, we'll feel bored. If the activity requires more energy than we have, we'll feel overwhelmed.

It's about balance, but it's also about focus. If we have the focus, we can summon the energy we need. Just by directing the energy onto an activity, we can cause the summoning of more energy. Energy always feeds itself and doesn't require anything but focus for direction and multiplication.

It's easier to move up from here because it's right on the verge of better-feeling environments and there is little resistance to weigh us down. There isn't much to do, except to shift focus. The energy is available to us to do whatever we choose.

There is no specific negativity or resistance that is pressing to be dealt with in this environment. It's general and not heavy. It's ready to be free flowing. It's waiting for our direction.

Sometimes, impatience and boredom both suggest a lack of feeling in control over our lives, environments, or circumstances.

When we don't know what to do, it might be because we think we can't do anything. Maybe we think we have no power to change the situation or environment. Maybe we feel stuck in a waiting room, or we have to do something we don't want to and therefore want the time to pass faster. The more we believe we have no control in our physical environment, the more likely we are to become bored or impatient.

Impatience doesn't make us ruminate over the past. It's really all about now and the speed in which now is moving. It feels like it's not moving fast enough for us. It's a form of denying the now, which is simply resistance. It's a form of rejecting what is in front of us for something we think is better. We want to get to the better, now.

Boredom, in the same way, feels like we're moving faster than everything else around us. We feel like we need to slow down our energy to match the environment, and we don't like that. So we either feel bored or impatient.

Boredom, however, can take us into the past because we might begin to daydream to pass time. We might start thinking about the past or start arguing with other people in our minds just to create some kind of excitement. We might even begin to create resistance because we are so bored.

This environment can ease so much resistance that we can become bored with ease and crave resistance again. This is why we might sometimes create unnecessary drama and problems just to have some stimulating activity to grab our focus and attention.

Sometimes we refer to that as being "drama queens" — also known as people who unnecessarily create problems because they like the excitement of it. The drama allows our energy to be focused on a problem, which feels much more stimulating than boredom.

The answer to boredom wouldn't be to find more ease. The ease is to help let go of the resistance, and once we do that, we don't require more ease. We require movement. We require focus.

The energy wants something exciting, something engaging, and we can easily create fun or excitement from this place.

We can easily get up and drive to the beach or call a friend and go to a movie. The resistance is low enough in this environment to begin the process of creating positive momentum and fun. Boredom can lead to a desire for fun.

Impatience wants us to get up and do something. It wants what it wants right now! It can't wait. It doesn't want to wait. Waiting is boring.

We can easily jump into a great flow of positivity and fun from this environment. We can also dip ourselves lower by adding resistance and causing problems for stimulation.

We can usually tell whether our impatience is eager, hopeful, or frustrating. That's how we will know in which direction we are moving energetically.

If we begin to build momentum in the direction of frustration, more and more things like it will transpire and make us frustrated. The energy will build on itself, and our impatience will eventually move down into frustration or even anger.

If we feel more hopefulness or playfulness in our impatience and boredom, then we'll easily find the means to entertain ourselves and find fun activities.

It's important to stay aware of the direction in which our emotions are moving. It's okay if we're in frustration right now if we can sense it's more of a hopeful frustration and not a raging one. We can feel a hopeless anger about the direction of our lives, or we can feel a hopeful anger.

If we can become more aware of the direction in which we're moving, we can adjust our emotions in the moment, thus changing the responses we get. All it takes is conscious effort on our parts. Just to step away for a moment and get clearer.

Impatience and boredom are good places to be in compared to the environments before it. There is very little resistance here, and all it requires is a little shift to move up. All we need is some focus to direct our energy where we would like it to be. That's all it takes.

What it Attracts:

The more impatient we are, the more likely we are to create delays. If our focus is on our lack of time, it will be filled with more delays. The less time you think you have, the less time you will have.

Our bus won't arrive on time, our plane will be delayed, we will be stuck in traffic, etc. The less time we have, the more we will create the delays that continue to take up our time.

It may sound unfair, but it's the fairest law of the universe; we get what we focus on. The more we rush something, the more we create delays to feed the feeling of rushing. The more we try to avoid fear, the more we create fearful situations. We create the thing we don't want because there's no such thing as holding an experience away from us. If you're holding it, it's in your experience.

The more we rush to eat to save time, the more likely we will be to spill it and then spend more time cleaning it up. The more we try to stay quiet so we don't wake someone up, the more likely we'll be to bump into things and make loud noises. The faster we want to get to work so we won't be reprimanded, the more likely we'll be to get stuck in traffic.

Energy goes where it is focused, even if the focus is on something unwanted. Energy doesn't judge whether something is good or bad for us; it gives us the match.

It calls its match to itself every time. Worry attracts more things to be worried about, frustration attracts more things to be frustrated about, fear attracts more things to be fearful of, and anger attracts more things to be angry about. Energy always creates cycles.

Creating, or attracting, from this environment is soft in nature. If we don't become frustrated with our impatience or boredom, we can find the right activities that will move us up into fun, excitement, and eagerness.

We don't have to try or apply effort here. We just have to follow the fun. We simply need to follow our bliss and not judge what comes our way. That's the best way we allow more.

Patience is really about understanding that we are getting exactly what we asked for in the moment we allow it to come. We might not necessarily get it in the order in which we want it, but we will get the aspects we are easy about first. We will get what we allow in first. We might not even realize we are allowing one part and resisting another.

If we were to get discouraged by seeing something coming that we didn't want, we would stop ourselves from getting any of it by introducing resistance through the feelings of disappointment, frustration, or disempowerment. Then, we would lower ourselves into more resistant environments where none of it is possible.

Most of the time, we get what we want out of order. We get what we're easiest about first. The timing may feel off with what we're getting and how we're getting it, but if we learn to relax more, we can enjoy the process. We can have faith that we are getting everything we asked for and allowed in. Energy doesn't lie; it doesn't trick us. We get more of what we feel. So if we feel faith and ease, we allow more of our other desires.

There is no rush because life is not a competition. No one wins at the end because there is no end. We are always learning, growing, and expanding. We are always moving from one form to another. We are always moving from one understanding to another. There is always growth within us and around us. Even the universe is always expanding and has no end point. We have no end point.

That's ultimately what it's about: the journey. Only the journey matters because only the journey exists. If we're impatient on the journey, if we're in pain or not enjoying it, then we're missing the point.

We're not ever going to find happiness or joy later because there is no later. All of those things exist now, in this moment, because now is what is creating our experiences. Later will just be another now. So take care of now.

Whether it's how we view the experiences of the past, or how we think about the future, it's all happening in the moment. We feel in the moment. We create in the moment.

We experience in the moment. Now is the magnet. Now is the creation. Now is the attraction. Now is where the power is. It's all happening now. Work on your feelings now, and later will be filled with more of the same.

Thought Clusters:

This environment is likely to compound a certain cluster of thoughts. One thought will trigger another like it, and that will trigger the next. We can spend minutes or hours thinking these types of thoughts, which feeds the energy of the environment. We rarely ever just think one of these thoughts—that's why they're called clusters. They usually pull each other into the thought process and are never isolated.

Thought clusters in boredom can be exactly or similar to the following:

"When am I going to get out of here?"
"Why am I even here?"
"What am I doing?"
"I should be doing something important."
"What should I do?"
"I don't want to do anything."
"Oh, who cares anyway?"
"I could be doing something fun."
"Stop wasting my time!"
"I'm bored."

Thoughts in boredom tend to be repetitive and loop in on themselves. It's the same with impatience. An impatient person might repeat the same lines over and over again like, "come on, come on." "Hurry up, hurry up." People who are bored might say they're bored six or seven times within the hour.

There isn't much room for something new or even something old. We probably won't dip down into the lower environments with the exception of frustration. We might become frustrated with our boredom and dip down a little just to create some excitement.

In this environment, the mind wants a specific focus to direct the energy. If one is not consciously made available, the mind will wander into daydreams or create unnecessary problems and dramas.

The mind is a powerful tool when it is focused. It can direct life-creating energy wherever we want. If we feel bored and unfocused, then we lack desire or passion. Either we are not allowing ourselves to want something more because we don't believe we'll get it, or we've become too comfortable in how things are and don't want to risk it. Maybe there's a little bit of fear present. Maybe there's too much comfort. Either way, we need something to feel passionate about. The best way to move up from this environment is through focus.

What To Do:

Impatience requires ease, but boredom requires action. This is the turning point of energy; the middle ground. All other environments before this one require ease, and all the environments above it require action. This is where the shift begins.

We usually do the opposite with these emotions. We sit around when we are bored, and we try to commit actions when we're impatient.

Boredom does not need easing; in this environment, ease only creates more boredom. If you try meditating when you're bored, you'll become annoyed. If you try acting from impatience, you'll create more delays.

Since boredom requires focused energy, you can start something that brings out a new passion. Do something you don't normally do. Work on that book you've always wanted to write. Take a swimming class. Try yoga. Learn a new language. Try something you've never done before, so it can engage your mind for the first time.

You can take an online class. Learn to bake. Join a gym. Take up a sport. Try something that challenges you mentally or physically. Start a new project. Go volunteer — there are plenty of people who need some of that extra energy you have.

Boredom is your energy saying, "I want to move! I want to grow! Direct me somewhere! Let me create!"

What ignites your passion? What gives you a sense of adventure? What would you like to do? What would you like to try? Work on that. Find something fun to do. Call a friend and train for a marathon together. Create a reading group. Start a business, take up a hobby, or learn a new skillset. Set a goal and work toward it. There's nothing like a mental challenge to keep us focused and dedicated. It can bring out passions we never knew we had.

For impatience, ease is the answer. A breathing meditation can be very helpful. As you're waiting or standing in line, count your breath. Count every time you inhale. Look around the room and see if you can play a game with yourself. How many blue items can you count? What don't you have that you would like? If you could redecorate the room, what would you change? Use your imagination.

A shift in focus can work very well. Start a conversation with someone nearby that brings you more ease. Distract the impatient energy by reading something—that's why waiting rooms carry magazines. A shift in focus can ease impatience. Call someone and talk about something else. Most importantly, breathe.

If you're feeling impatience with your life in general, any action you commit will only prolong the process and frustrate you. The only way to find ease is to accept the process of your life instead of trying to rush it. There are components you need before you can get to where you want to be. If you didn't, you would already be there. You have to reach those first. Maybe one of them is patience.

Once you have all of the components, your goals will become easier to accomplish. That's what this is all about: ease. If you allow the process to unfold naturally, it will take you through the easiest path. If you fight it, struggle with it, or try to force it, then you will only create more resistance for yourself.

Take a deep breath, and let it go. You are smarter, stronger, and wiser for everything you've gone through. You are also clearer than you've ever been. You have a much better idea of who you are and what you want from your life.

Maybe it wasn't easy before; that's okay, too. The past is in the past, and we're not going to judge it anymore. We're not going to turn it into a tragedy, and we're not going to turn it into our golden years. We're not going to be sad about it because that changes nothing in the past and only creates more of the same in the now.

It's all about now because now is where your point of power is. Now you know better, and that's all that matters.

Environment 8:
The Optimists
Hopeful, Content, Acceptance, Peace

The Energy of The Optimists:

This is the environment of positive expectation, as well as peace. This is the beginning of the free-flowing energy shift. From here, the energy moves much faster in the direction of joy and can easily sweep us up into it. It can happen in a matter of a few seconds of feeling hopeful, which is the softest feeling in this environment.

One hopeful thought can lead to an eager one, which can lead to a joyful one. A hopeful thought can make us feel more content in our lives, which can bring us more peace. Additionally, this is the environment of acceptance, which also brings peace. Here, we are flowing with the stream of life. We are not resisting or fighting anything; not our thoughts, not our feelings, not circumstances, not others, and not life. We feel peaceful about where we are in life and hopeful about where we're going.

This doesn't mean everything is perfect in our lives. It doesn't mean we have no problems or setbacks. It simply means we have learned how to manage our thoughts and emotions enough to shift them. It means we have build trust and confidence in our abilities. We accept responsibility for our emotions and actions. We feel confident in our ability to take care of ourselves and reach our goals. We believe in ourselves. We have faith in ourselves. We trust life.

We might be in this environment generally or with one or two aspects of our lives. It's possible to feel this way with your family but be in a lower environment at work, or vice versa. It's also possible that most aspects are in this environment, while only one or two aspects are in lower environments. Optimism can be a general mindset, or it can be dependent on the conditions of each aspect.

If we practice enough in this environment, then we can become experts in not allowing the conditions to dictate our feelings or responses. We can learn to master our lives through mastering our emotions.

Faith becomes activated in this environment, as well. Perhaps we haven't yet reached our goals or achieved what we set out to do. However, there is a level of faith that allows us to continue forward with positive expectation. This is the turning point from faith to belief.

Once faith becomes belief, there is no stopping the energy from coming back into our experience. Once we know — not just hope or have faith — once we believe that it's a sure thing, then it is. Then we will be presented with

Emily Maroutian

sign after sign, opportunity after opportunity to reach our desires.

Knowing pulls us up through the environments much faster. You might only spend a few minutes in despair before your strong belief or faith kicks in. It expedites the energy and experience. Hope helps us to see it, and faith begins the process of belief. As we inch closer and see more evidence of it through our faith, we move into belief, and then it must happen.

If at any time we were to introduce doubt or resistance, we would sink into lower environments. However, all it would take is a quick shift in perspective to bring us back into hope. As we hope, we expect more. As we expect, we see. As we see, we believe.

Beliefs are created through the aspects we focus on, how we interpret them, and how we feel about them. Later, when we look at similar aspects, it triggers the interpretation and feeling automatically, creating a reinforcing cycle. Interrupting any of the three steps will help shift beliefs because a belief is simply the repetition of thoughts. Those thoughts create more of the same thoughts, and it becomes a filter through which we view the world. The more evidence we see in the form of experiences, the more we believe those thoughts are true.

We can easily do this in other environments, as well. We can create beliefs in depression, victimhood, or rage by thinking repetitive thoughts in those environments and then respond to the feedback that comes through those emotions. Once we do that a few times, it becomes a belief. It becomes a fact we accept about life or the world.

So many of our current beliefs are nothing more than repetitive thoughts we began thinking as children. We observed the world around us, we had some feelings about it, and then we declared our judgments as facts. Most of the time, we can't even see them as changeable because we decided a very long time ago that it was the reality of the world or our lives.

The good news is that we can do the same now with the feelings we want to feel. We don't have to be on default feeling mode and just recycle the old thoughts and feelings. We can start today, and we can start by feeling hopeful. If this book does nothing more than offer you some hope, that's good enough.

We are more aware now than we were yesterday. That's a hopeful thought. We know better today. There are so many resources all around us. We can search for ways to relax. We can learn exercises and techniques anytime we want. We are surrounded by knowledge. And the best part is that we don't even have to learn a bunch of new things— we just need to relax most of the time.

As we relax and find more ease, we naturally become more hopeful about our lives and future. The more hopeful we become, the more we begin to see it in the feedback we receive from our experiences with the world and other people. If we practice enough hope, it will become a belief.

Hope and belief are in the same environment, but the movement of energy is at different speeds. Knowing will move us up much faster than just hoping. They're both moving us in the direction we want; it's just that one moves us faster.

The difference is that hope is a calm stream, and belief is a raging rapid. There is no stopping it. Once we're in it, we go where it takes us, regardless of whether we want to. This is why beliefs are powerful; they are creating our experiences every day, and we don't even realize that we turned on the water. We created the rapids.

We let go of most of our resistance when we believe that something is going to happen. We relax into what we know. We let the rapid take us without resistance or a fight because we accept where we're headed. It brings us a peace of mind to know we're going to get there. It brings contentment, and that is what moves the free-flowing energy even faster.

Also, when we know, we rarely have to consciously think about it. It just feels normal. A belief feels easy because it has become a part of reality. Most of the time, we're not even aware of it.

When we have a belief, there is rarely any conscious need to plan it out or get consensus from others. We don't call up our friend to ask if the sky is blue today. We believe and expect it to be; therefore, we don't even think about it. Most beliefs aren't even in our consciousness. Because they are accepted as facts, we don't think twice about it.

We have similar beliefs in our lives about who we are, what we are capable of, and what our futures hold. We are walking into those futures through those beliefs without even realizing it. We are creating our futures from emotional environments we no longer want to be in but have accepted as unchangeable facts.

We can do that with hope, and peace, and happiness, as well. We can practice these thoughts and feelings until they become a normal aspect of our lives. If we can hang around in this environment a little more than we did yesterday, we'll be on our way there. That's all it takes: a little bit of hope.

This is the environment of ease. Every single environment before it has been leading to this one. All of the other processes and activities were designed to bring us here, to a place of ease, peace, contentment, and acceptance.

If we stayed here and didn't move up, our lives would be just fine. We might get bored or impatient from time to time, dipping just a little bit to the previous environment, but ultimately, we will become eager and enthusiastic easily.

Most religions and religious practices are designed to bring us here. Meditation's sole purpose is to bring us into this environment of peace and contentment.

It's hard to imagine that there is more than this when we are here. We feel so fulfilled and peaceful that we don't even want to ask for much more.

We can see the next step in our lives, and we believe that it will happen. We move little by little. Step by step, we advance. We feel no particular rush, but we feel motivated enough in our everyday lives.

The contentment and acceptance of our lives is strong in this environment. We have hope for a better future, and things feel better and brighter. This is a wonderful environment to be in, and if we can practice the energy of it every day, we can live a satisfied life.

What it Attracts:

This environment sets us up for pleasant and spontaneous meetings and opportunities with others. One hopeful encounter can lead to another and another. Hope attracts more experiences that validate our hopeful state. The more we see, the more we believe. As we believe, it becomes easier to feel hopeful about our future.

As we generally feel more hopeful, we begin to attract feedback along the way, which reassures us that we are on the right track. They are the universe's breadcrumbs that keep us hopeful on the journey to what we want. Most people called it synchronicity.

This environment is the beginning process of free-flowing energy, which creates positive-feeling synchronicity. Here, we match up with the good-feeling experiences that perpetuate our good feelings. Events line up for us in an almost perfect sequence with one thing leading to another and another to bring us what we desire.

We also begin to feel the resonance within us when we think of something and then it appears immediately in our experience. We think of someone, and they call us in that moment. We have a dream about something, and then experience it in our day.

We can feel the ease in which we attract and create in our lives because they are mostly positive-feeling experiences with little or no effort. They create a very specific feeling that has only been previous described as synchronicity.

It is an energetic resonance between the thought/feeling and the encounter, experience, or thing. It is an energetic match that we can feel as we experience it.

We can also feel that resonance with the new people we meet. Most people in this environment feel that resonance with others on a daily basis. People who are frequently in lower environments might feel that connection once or twice as they come into this environment and then mistake it for a soul-mate connection. When it happens rarely for people, it feels like luck. It feels special.

In this environment, we feel that connection with multiple people frequently, almost on a daily basis. It can happen with the grocery store bag boy or the woman sitting next to us on a bench. People can feel like familiar life-long friends within a few minutes of meeting each other. Everyone begins to feel like a soul mate.

The encounters don't have to be romantic in nature. They just feel deep, connected, and synchronistic. We often find ourselves saying, "Oh. You, too?"

Within a few minutes of conversation, we find out they work in our same field or maybe the field we want work in. They have already started the diet we want to be on. They had the same illness but recovered. They end up bringing us hope for our journey or an opportunity for our future. This is how we know we are energetically moving forward in the direction of ease and free-flowing energy. It feels right. We feel as though we are on the right path.

There is no wrong direction or path. While this environment makes us feel as though we are moving in the right direction, that doesn't mean there is a wrong one. There is the right direction that feels easy or the right direction with resistance. As the saying goes, all roads lead to Rome.

Moving down into a lower environment is not wrong. It just adds more resistance while we're on our journey. That doesn't mean it's a negative journey or the wrong direction—just one full of resistance and effort. It's a harder version of our path, but not because it was destined to us by a higher power. It's because we choose our emotions, which sets up the path.

There are many roads with different degrees of difficulty on the way, but it's the same destination. The people we meet on the way all vary, depending on which path we choose. The path sets up the obstacles, the people, the loves, and everything else.

This is why when we change our emotions and environments, we lose friends or lovers. They can't take our path with us if they no longer match up with it. There will be other friends and lovers on each path; no one walks alone. Even when we are depressed or physically alone, we still have people who are matches to our energy.

When we grow together, we walk similar paths. When we grow apart, we take other paths. That doesn't mean we won't ever see them again. There is no loss, wrong direction, or negative energy. We can choose to go down any path we feel inclined at any moment. We can shift at any time by shifting our emotions.

There is no rush. There is no wrong. The feeling of resistance creates the feeling of negativity but there is no negative or wrong energy. Only free-flowing energy and energy full of resistance, which feels negative. We are in control of our emotions, therefore we are in control of our paths.

All we have to do is relax and follow our instincts as it unfolds before us. The path of optimism is one of the nicest routes. Enjoy it.

Thought Clusters:

This environment is likely to compound a certain cluster of thoughts. One thought will trigger another like it, and that will trigger the next. We can spend minutes or hours thinking these types of thoughts, which feeds the energy of the environment. We rarely ever just think one of these thoughts — that's why they're called clusters. They usually pull each other into the thought process and are never isolated.

Thought clusters in optimism can be exactly or similar to the following:

"Things will get better; they always do."

"I can work through this. "
"It's possible."
"Others have been successful — so can I."
"Things can turn around for me easily."
"It's not that bad."
"The answer will come to me."
"I feel better now."
"I can do this."
"Life gets better and better."

Thoughts in optimism always leave us feeling better about whatever we are experiencing. It is the environment of positive expectation. If we feel any kind of relief from any other environment, we can easily jump to hope from there.

Just saying something like, "I feel better now" is a hopeful thought. To acknowledge the good feeling gives hope for more. There is positive expectation that things might work out. This optimistic point of view sets us up to see it all around us.

What To Do:

This is a great environment to be in. It's a wonderful home environment, and a lot of spiritual books teach that this is the place in which we aspire to be. Peace is the ultimate goal for those who have experienced great pain, suffering, or illness.

You can continue to have faith, hope, and peace and live a good life. If you find yourself here and are content with your life, then you don't need to do anything other than what you have already been doing. You will move up naturally because the energy will flow and speed up.

Keep paying attention to hopeful synchronicities. Keep your focus on the wellness in your body. Enjoy the space around you. Make appreciation lists and keep a gratitude journal. Consider writing thank-you cards to the people who make your life easier. Enjoy the opportunities for laughter and fun. Enjoy your friends and family. Love your life and just keep doing what you're already doing.

Pay attention to the areas in your life where solutions are easily available and things work out well for you. Keep your focus on the wellbeing around you. Follow your bliss, and see where it leads you. Have some faith in how things are turning out. Believe that it's all for the best.

Pay attention to your passions. Find what wakes you up and makes you come alive. Keep yourself open to causes that would greatly benefit from your energy and optimism. Allow yourself to be in service of others, and you will move into gratitude and appreciation. Keep your focus on the positive end results, but also believe that they are possible. Your passion will move you forward. You will feel a strong sense of fulfillment and joy. You will feel your heart expanding, and you will feel more purposeful in your life.

You don't have to do much of anything. When you're happy, you will find things to be passionate about. When you feel hopeful, you will find things to be happy about. This environment makes it easy to move into eagerness and enthusiasm. You might get super happy about your new grapefruit or a pair of shoes. It doesn't matter what it is, as long as the emotion is a good one.

This environment is on the brink of eagerness, so feeling hopeful can easily make us feel eager. We can jump back and forth among the top three environments. Just as it was easy to go from depression to shame to revenge to blame, it's even easier to go from hope to eagerness to joy.

When you find yourself moving up naturally to the next environment, be easy about it. You might feel eager for a little while, but then you might calm down into hopefulness or peace. Don't think of it as a drop. Think of it as a settling in. Think of it as coming home from an exciting day and feeling generally peaceful and relaxed about your life. You may be eager about tomorrow, but right now you feel good.

That's good enough.

Environment 9:
The Movers
Enthusiasm, Eagerness, Passion

The Energy of The Movers:

Movers tend to be people who are constantly inspired into action. Our actions from this environment don't feel like effort or struggle. It feels easy because passion moves us. We tend to be hard workers, but our work never feels hard. We can spend ten hours working on something and still have energy left over for more. In fact, the more work we do, the more energized we feel.

No one else, in any other environment, can do so much while being so focused in so little time as someone who is passionately tuned into what they love or enjoy doing.

We can accomplish more through passion than we ever can through effort. Moreover, we will have much more energy left over at the end of the day. We will feel fulfilled and ready to do more. We will wake up the next day and look forward to doing more work.

Passion will feed our energy because the more we use it, the more it replenishes. However, effort is depleting. The more we use it, the less we have to use the next time around. We don't even want to use it the next time because it's an exhausting process. It becomes a struggle with our energy because we are trying to commit action to compensate for energy that isn't there. We are forced to work "hard" to accomplish anything.

We can become resentful, angry, or feel like the victim of a boss or our parents who "forced" us into the career. We will search for others to blame. Our energy will deplete, and we won't want to do much of anything else. "Hard" work is hard on energy because there isn't enough of it to begin with.

We can perform the same exact physical task and have different energy levels and different results. If at one time we use force and another we use ease, we will create different results. We can try to make things happen, or we can allow it. We can have a particular way through the path for which we are fighting, or we can be open to changes and detours that use better parts of the path.

Ease is flexible. It's free flowing and always reaches its destination without force. In this sense, it's like a flowing stream. If there are a few rocks in the way, water simply goes around it. It finds a crack, a hole, a way to get to its destination. It doesn't have to force anything. It doesn't try; it doesn't apply effort. Passion is never forceful; that's rage and anger. That's frustration and control, which often gets confused for passion.

Imagine if you stopped and tried to break or demolish every rock on your path. You would be tired and unmotivated. You would waste your time and energy by using force.

Passion makes everything feel easy. This is why we can look at someone and marvel at their ability to work so hard and accomplish so much. It almost looks easy to us. However, if we were to attempt it, we might struggle. We might have a hard time. That's because it's not our passion. We would be forcing it if we were to do it.

We can't find passion in doing other people's work. We have to feel a part of the work we are doing to feel that level of passion. It must be our passion.

A leader who knows how to inspire passion will tie their vision with our own so well that every action we take will feel like we are working toward our own goal. They will show us that our vision and their vision are really one in the same. Then, we're not working FOR them — we're working WITH them, on something we both believe in. It creates a level of passion that is unparalleled.

We can also feel passionate about our meatloaf, or our children, or the dogs. We can feel passionate about playing the guitar or collecting stamps. We can feel passionate about anything we love.

Passion is a powerful movement of energy because it is a powerful focuser of energy. It can speed up the process of any project because it narrows our attention and only allows us to see what is right in front of us. We only see our project, our lover, or our hobby. Hours can pass, and we will still be immersed in it with enthusiasm and energy.

Eagerness is the softer version of the energy. It usually comes before full-on passion. It can remain throughout the process but almost always comes before it.

When we begin to feel enthusiasm and eagerness about something we haven't begun yet, there is a great possibility that we can become passionate about it. If we can stay focused on what we are doing or are going to do, we can conjure up a lot of passion.

It's usually in these early stages that we begin to look at the aspects we don't want or don't like and introduce resistance into our energy. We begin to split our focus and slow down the momentum of the energy.

Passion becomes hard work when we focus more on what we don't like or don't want to do. A simple shift in perspective can change the feeling of our work. Purpose can turn into burden. The work will stay the same, but the feeling behind it will change, thus changing the energy and trajectory of the project.

However, if we can stay around this area and only dip into hope, then we can get our passion and enthusiasm back easily. We must find ways to remind ourselves of what our vision was and why we began in the first place. There is already momentum there that was built a while back. If we can remember the feeling, we can bring back the momentum, and everything will begin to flow easily again.

What it Attracts:

Environments 8 through 10 are various speeds of free-flowing energy. Environments 1 through 6 are various magnitudes of resistance to the free-flowing energy, with the first environment holding the most amount of resistance. The more resistance there is, the slower the energy flows.

Passion is the middle environment of free-flowing energy. It's easy to jump up and down within these three environments, 8-10, feeling enthusiastic one moment and peaceful the next. Feeling passionate can attract hopeful and joyful encounters.

While these three environments are positive and free flowing in nature, they can also bring up issues and problems that began in lower environments. When this occurs, it's not a sign that things are beginning to turn back down; it is an opportunity to see those issues within these environments. It is an opportunity to shift them into a better-feeling place.

However, if we are to use the presence of them as an excuse to dip down emotionally, then we will meet the problem where it is instead of bringing the problem where we are. If we are to ever feel complete or closure about it, we must lift the problem into one of these three environments.

We have to bring it to the point where we either feel hopeful about its resolution, find peace with it, feel enthusiastic about its unraveling, feel love for the person involved, or feel joyful that we are able to learn from it. There are many avenues, ways, and emotions we can use to shift resistant issues into a free-flowing energy.

Within these three environments, everything we felt about old ideas, relationships, jobs, people will come to the surface because it no longer wants to stay in resistance. When our energy is freer, our perspective wants to be, as well. And if we continue to see the old issues with old eyes, we will pull ourselves back into lower environments and introduce resistance into our new endeavors.

Every belief we have will show up one way or another when we are working on a project that we are passionate about, or a new relationship we love, or anything else that inspires free-flowing energy.

If we have feelings of unworthiness, they will come up through an encounter with a client or a business partner. If we feel shame, it will come up as an incident with our lover. If we believe we aren't good enough, we will see it in the feedback we get from others.

Our fast-flowing energy brings to the surface all of the things we previously left in lower environments. When we focus on those old problems, we shift our current focus into lower-environment feelings, and that begins to affect our current projects, relationships, and endeavors.

Just by focusing on something from the past that didn't feel good, we change our energy in the present and introduce resistance into our current endeavors. This is very common. We go with the emotion from the past because it feels familiar and has momentum. It's easier to jump into those old feelings and problems because we've practiced them more.

However, if we stay conscious, we can pull the problem into our new emotion instead of allowing the old emotion to pull the new situation into it.

What we attract from this environment is positive in nature, even when they are the old problems that don't feel positive yet. They are on their way to catch up to us and our new energy. They are coming to us to find a new home environment.

Most things we attract here will continue to fuel our passion, enthusiasm, and eagerness. If we can look at those old issues with the same enthusiasm and hopefulness, they will work themselves out with little effort or work from us.

Thought Clusters:
This environment is likely to compound a certain cluster of thoughts. One thought will trigger another like it,

and that will trigger the next. You can spend minutes or hours thinking these types of thoughts, which feeds the energy of the environment. We rarely ever just think one of these thoughts — that's why they're called clusters. They usually pull each other into the thought process and are never isolated.

Thought clusters in passion can be exactly or similar to the following:

"Life is so exciting!"
"I can't wait to do that!"
"Wow, did four hours pass already?"
"I'm not even tired!"
"I love to work on my projects!"
"I feel so purposeful!"
"I feel energetic!"
"I feel so alive!"
"I feel so high off of life!"
"It feels good to work!"

Thoughts in passion and enthusiasm come fast without filtration. They are similar to aggression in that sense, but the exact opposite in energy. They're both fast moving energies except passion is just one step away from joy.

We might not even have any other thoughts than those pertaining specifically to what we're passionate about. This environment has the most powerful form of focus. It can draw more and more thoughts like it, building up great momentum in a short time.

The greatest movers and shakers who have ever lived spent a lot of time in this environment. It's the energy of their passions that have moved their projects and causes into the hearts of millions of people. It can be that easy if we stay focused on our passions.

What To Do:

There isn't much to do in this environment because it takes care of itself. Passion feeds passion, and energy becomes available as it is needed.

It is only one small step from joy, freedom, love, and empowerment. Our only job in this environment is to continue to stay focused in our passions and allow it to empower us and bring us joy.

Passion without fulfillment is draining. It becomes hard work. So it's important to feel fulfilled in our work. It's important to love what we do and experience some joy from our endeavors.

It is possible to feel passionate and eager but not feel free or peaceful. We can become trapped in our passions or consumed by them. We can run our bodies down and become ill. We can exhaust ourselves.

We have to honor our body. If it says eat, then we eat. If it says more sleep, we give it more sleep. It's important to listen to our bodies in this environment because the energy can carry us far in a short time, but it can also burn us out physically.

If we don't honor our bodies consciously, we will end up introducing resistance just to slow ourselves down. We will get a cold or a stomach virus. We will create something in our bodies that will put on the brakes and force us to relax and heal.

Take a few minutes to meditate — it doesn't have to be for a long time. Five or ten minutes is enough. Go for a short walk before dinner. Eat more foods that give your body natural fuel. Drink more water. Take calming baths. Give your body relaxation from time to time.

If you take care of your body in this environment, you can streamline anything you are working on super fast without burning out or becoming ill.

As you build more momentum in this environment and honor your body in the process, you will feel more purposeful in how you live your life. Then, it's a quick jump into joy and empowerment.

Your only job is to let it happen.

Environment 10:
The Aligned
Joy, Empowerment, Freedom, Love

The Energy of The Aligned:

This environment feels indescribable when we are in it. It sweeps us up into its powerful energy, and it offers us a completely different perspective than any other environment before it. It changes everything. The words joy, empowerment, freedom, and love can't be compared to how they feel. They have the power to radically alter our whole life and how we interact with everything and everyone in it.

The energy of alignment is the highest frequency possible. This is the "god" space. This is the most powerful energy because it is full and complete free-flowing energy. This is the energy that creates worlds. There is zero resistance here. It feels unifying, light, and uplifting. We have a much broader view of the world and our lives from this perspective. We see connection and oneness in everything.

We also feel a lot of love for everything from this perspective. Not just for the things that are easy to love, and not just for the things that "deserve" love. We feel it for everything because there's an understanding of the interconnection of all things. There is no judgment on things being "right" or "wrong." It all feels connected. It all feels like one.

Alignment is oneness. There is no duality in it. From this environment, "others" are not others. They are our shadow selves, our mirrors, our disowned parts. They are a great benefit to us. They are here to show us where our wound is and what needs to be healed. In this environment, there is only love and what needs love.

Every other environment holds some kind of duality. There is the victim and aggressor, the bored and the passionate, the peaceful and the rageful. Yes, love has hate, empowerment has disempowerment, joy has depression, but none of them exist as a duality in this environment. They only exist as a duality in hate, disempowerment, and depression. In other words, those negative feelings take on new meaning here.

In this environment, we are compassionate and wise. We've learned many lessons from other environments, and it has come together to bring us a deep understanding. We know what it feels like to be in all of the environments, and we are not going to judge others for where they are currently. We are not going to look down on anyone. We feel love and understanding for them. We are open and ready to share our experiences and love with them. We are ready to give. We are ready to heal. We are ready to accept others. Lover and loved are one.

We don't place outside conditions on our feeling love within ourselves. The outside world can be a chaotic mess, and we will continue the love we feel. Our love is not dependent on other people's behavior or on circumstances working out for us.

We don't feel the need to judge others and then inflict punishment to make things right. This might make us seem indifferent to others who believe that punishment is the only way to balance things or get justice. That's okay.

We can seem like aliens to others who won't be able to understand what we do or why we do it. And if we were to try to explain ourselves, we would receive a debate or argument back, which would cause us to leave this environment. Needing to justify or explain this environment forces us to leave it. We can only share it and hope others are inspired.

This is the Jesus and Buddha space. When we feel all four of the emotions from this environment, then we enter the "god" space.

This is also the space in which a loving teacher can offer us a way out of the hate, anger, pain, and suffering. It doesn't have to be Jesus or Buddha specifically. Teachers take on many forms. It's not who that matters most, it's the energetic space, the environment that heals.

They can come and offer you love and freedom, but if you won't leave Environment 3 because you feel angry all the time, then nothing will happen. No one can force you anywhere. People can be guides, they can be catalysts, and they can help you, but only if you're willing to go.

We can enter this space, as well. We don't do it as often as Jesus and Buddha did, but we do it in small increments.

We feel some love for this one person, but only if they behave as we want them to. We feel some freedom at the beach or the park. We feel joy for buying a new item or for getting some extra money. We feel these feelings, but they are conditional and limited. To enter into the god space, all of these feelings must be unconditional.

Jesus was betrayed and beaten, and still he loved those who betrayed and beat him. Buddha saw death, sickness, and suffering around him, and still he maintained his alignment. The love, joy, and freedom they felt were not dependent on their shackles, their wounds, or their treatment. They understood on a different level. They understood on this level.

From this perspective, we understand that people in lower environments have to defend their limitations because it's comforting. It has nothing to do with us; it's about their own emotional needs. "Father, forgive them; for they know not what they do." Jesus prayed for the men who crucified him. How many times have you prayed for someone who hurt you? How many times have you understood why they hurt you? If you're not in this environment, all of this is going to sound crazy, offensive, or upsetting.

Since energy feeds itself, no amount of aligned words can reach someone who can't hear it. It will only feed their anger or sadness or doubt. Jesus himself couldn't reach everybody with love and forgiveness; you won't either.

We can only see as far as our emotional environments will allow. In Environments 1 through 6, we can only see as far as our resistance will allow us to see. If we have more momentum in higher environments, we might be able to attract an aligned or enlightened individual who can support us or guide us up higher when we are depressed or angry.

We can be in lower environments and attract teachers who can support us. However, we must, to some degree, believe and allow their entrance into our lives or else they'll feel annoying or insane to us.

Teachers and supporters can come through the appearance of a book, a seminar, a conversation at the bus stop, a movie, an article online, etc. We are always attracting from our level of belief and our degree of resistance to something. We can be depressed and still believe that a spiritual teacher might be able to help us. In this case, we can be in a depressed emotional environment about most everything else in our lives but feel hopeful toward a teacher. That tiny crack of hope is enough to bring an opportunity for a teacher into our lives. The opportunity will attract a teacher who will help lift the rest of our energy into a hopeful environment.

In this environment, we are the teachers. We are the healers and the helpers. We see more clearly, more openly, and with more love and understanding. We see those who are depressed and aggressive not as people who are lazy with their lives or predators that need punishment. We understand their pain, their journey, and their environment. We want to help move them up into love, freedom, and joy. We don't want others to suffer.

We feel compassion for others, but not in the way that changes our energy to match theirs. We don't lower ourselves into their pain; instead, we uplift them into our alignment. We hold the vision for their wellbeing and support them until they are able to see it themselves. We become the teachers, the uplifters, and the supporters. It comes naturally from this environment, and we are not drained by it. We don't exhaust ourselves. We don't force it; we allow it. The energy just flows. It replenishes itself.

We don't become quick to anger when we are presented with problems or the horrors of the world. We know that there's more power in passion and alignment. We know that change happens through focusing on what we do want instead of being angry about what we don't.

One of the common misconceptions about progress is that we can only be productive when we are angry. Anger will move the energy forward but only if we were on environments below it. From higher environments, anger will feel draining. It only empowers us if we felt disempowered before. In which case, it's healthy and necessary. No emotion is wrong. They are all necessary.

If we are aligned, we will not engage with others in an angry manner to validate our positions or beliefs. We will understand this process and not feel angry with them for seeking comfort in the familiar lower environments. We won't judge or blame them for trying to pull anger out of us so that we feel familiar to them. We will hold steady in our alignment because it is more powerful and beneficial for us than anger.

We also won't need to forgive others for trying to trigger us because we will have a better understanding of energy overall. We don't need to forgive anyone because we don't condemn or blame them in the first place. To do that, we would have to dip down into lower environments.

Without blame, there is no need for forgiveness. This perspective holds an understanding that doesn't require blame. That will sound utterly ridiculous to someone who is currently in a lower environment.

If you feel as though you need to go through a process of forgiveness to release resistance and allow ease, then you are welcome to try anything that works for you. That won't take place in this environment because there is no resistance here. Forgiveness will help release the resistance and move us to this perspective, but from here, we don't forgive because there is no resistance. It's not even an issue anymore. The only time we will need to forgive others is if they require it, not us.

While there are multiple ways in which I can explain this environment, the people who are in it won't need it, and those who are not won't truly understand it. When you are aligned, you will know. There will be no mistaking it, and you won't need an explanation. You will feel free and expansive. You will understand others, life, and the world from another level. You will have an inclusive, wider view of everything. You will feel the connection to all things.

You will feel love and appreciation. And in fact, appreciation is the same energy as love. They are interchangeable. It is impossible to truly feel the appreciation of something and not feel love for it.

When you are here, you will know. You will feel it in your body, in your heart, and you will see it in your life. When you are not here, you will also know. We can feel the resistance in our energy just as much as we can feel the lack of it.

We can feel the freedom just as powerfully as the lack of it. We can feel the love just as powerfully as the absence of it. When we're not aligned, we can feel it. But when our energy is free flowing at the highest frequency without any resistance, it is incomparable.

What it Attracts:

Even though this is the natural state of energy, we usually spend less time here than any other environment. Our energy normally experiences resistance at least several times a day based on our thinking and judgments. We bring it into our energy by observing life's contrasts and focusing more on the problems, pain, and the lacks.

How fast it takes for us to align again will depend on our momentum. We might get lost in the conflicts around us and allow fear to encompass our experiences. We might even forget about alignment. We might also lose the desire for it momentarily.

When we are deep in anger, we forget hope. When we are depressed, we forget alignment. The current dominant environment will overtake our experiences and change the way we see life. If we dip down, we won't care much about alignment.

Alignment has two forms of attraction. It attracts matches on the same level like success, happiness, fun, opportunities, wealth, health, joy, and freedom. Or it attracts openings for us to bring those things to others who are ready for it—or in other words, people who have "asked" for what we have to offer. In this environment, what we give to others is never a loss to us. What we give always enhances us. By feeding others, we feed ourselves.

You will attract people who feel good to you in either regard. People who want to bring you opportunities for the things you love, desire, or need. People with good energy who want to have fun with you. Surprises that delight you. You will attract random gifts and love and exciting adventures. Paths will open where none had been before.

In this environment, we don't see problems the way everyone else in other environments do. In fact, we see them as opportunities; opportunities for growth, for change, for more compassion or love, for teachers, for supporters, for uniters.

We notice a problem only for a short period of time because then our mind switches to the possibilities for a solution. We don't ruminate over issues. We don't stay stuck in a problem. We don't get angry over it; we don't hate ourselves for having it. We simply allow ourselves to find the solution.

However, as we focus on the pains and troubles of the world, we forget about the abundance of wellness in it. We shift our focus, and that shifts the way we begin to feel. At the end of the day, we focus on the one file that caused problems instead of the forty that ran smoothly and easily.

We remember the people who annoyed us and took too long while we were standing in line, and we forget about the people who were helpful and kind. We don't pay attention to the ease in which we arrived safely at home and focus more on the one car that wouldn't drive fast enough or the red lights that slowed us down.

We allow the ease to slip into the background of our awareness and only focus on the issues that come up because we believe it's a matter of survival. We are hardwired to survive, and we think as long as we're anxious, as long as we worry, we'll see the problem coming before it has a chance to get us.

We think that if we don't see the problem coming, then it will destroy us before we have a chance to react. We are always waiting for the sneak attack from life, almost as if we're at war with life and we have to be a few steps ahead of it or else death, pain, or illness will win. We forget alignment, peace, and hope. We forget the natural balance of life. We forget that up has down and inside has outside.

We forget that experiencing one thing doesn't mean the opposite doesn't exist. We will experience both, and we will be okay.

We become afraid to be happy because we think we will put our guard down. We fear feeling comfortable and safe. We think it makes us vulnerable. When we narrow our perspective only to see the rare few around us who aren't well or safe, it skews our whole view of the abundant wellness, cooperation, and goodness that is all around us. This ends up sucking us right into the environment of vulnerability, Environment 2.

More things run smoothly than not. There are more well people in the world than sick. More children are safe in schools than not. There are more good things in our lives than not. If we focus more on the not, we won't even see the good.

While there are accidents, sicknesses, and incidents that compete for our attention on a daily basis, they are not more powerful than the wellness that surrounds us. There is more wellness in our bodies than not. If that statement weren't true, we would be dead. There is more balance in our bodies, more organs running smoothly, and more cells doing their job than not. If they didn't, we couldn't function at all and couldn't live. There is so much more wellness around us. We can be in an active warzone and still have more wellness than not.

The world is a good place. Can it be better? Always. In this environment, we are in the best position to make it better. We are walking problem solvers. We radiate joy, love, support, peace, kindness, and compassion. We fill the gaps and lacks. We are beacons lighting up the small dark corners of our little piece of the world.

We are what the world needs more of, but we don't focus on the lacks here. We know that focus is power and we don't offer problems our power. If we focused on the negatives, we wouldn't last in this environment very long. When Buddha spoke with an unenlightened person, he saw the possibility of their enlightenment. When Jesus spoke with a sick person, he saw the possibility of their wellness. They did not focus on the negativity that existed in the present moment; they focused on the possibility that was coming.

The only time we are able to see the world for what it truly is, is when we are in this environment, which is why I keep referring to it more as a perspective than an environment. Our experiences and the possibilities that exist within them are all dependent on our perspective of our experiences, which depend on how we feel overall, which depends on what we choose to focus on.

From a more free-flowing state, like the top three environments, we are more likely to line up with the answers because we don't view unwanted events and circumstances as problems that need tackling and beating up. We don't view anything as an obstacle that requires effort and struggle to win over. We don't charge at anything head first to become victorious.

If we are constantly looking at the problems and feeling angry about them, we are more likely to feed the energy of the problem because energy always feeds energy. The more we struggle to find something, the less likely we are to see that it is right in front of us. Ease reveals the way, not struggle.

Depression or anger don't solve problems; they just keep the focus on it. It makes us think we're being productive by constantly looking at the problem and judging it. However, very little advancement happens from that state as compared to the advancement that is possible from a free-flowing emotional state.

Even though negativity pushes us to want change, we're almost never in the right state to enact the appropriate change. The options and opportunities that are available from lower environments are limited at best. Everything we do there is meant to bring us up here. This is why relief exercises are so important. They move us up to environments that help us become more productive and valuable.

It's not about sticking our heads in the sand and allowing horrible things to happen in the world. It's about not acting from the same energy that created the problem in the first place, which is usually anger, hate, blame, and shame. Bringing the same energy to the problem only feeds the problem. You can't ease anger through anger. You can't fix hate with hate. You must bring new energy to a problem, or else it can't move.

We are more likely to see the solutions when we are aligned. We'll see avenues and paths we hadn't considered before. People will come into our lives offering new strategies. We'll watch a program that answers our questions. We'll bump into solution after solution.

Sometimes, we'll find that once we're in a better-feeling place, we don't even want to think about it anymore. It's almost as if the problem disappears. The energy of the problem doesn't match our energy anymore. That's because most problems are environment based and once we leave the environment, we leave the problem.

Then, when we return to the lower environment, we are met with the problem once again. After Environment 7, all problems become hopeful avenues of possibility. All problems cease being problems and become opportunities for change. It doesn't FEEL the same. There is no need to feel defensive or aggressive. There is no victim or aggressor. There is none of that thinking, especially from this perspective.

In this environment, we are more likely to see things as wanted or unwanted. And we are less likely to argue or fight against the unwanted. We are more likely to just let it go with ease. This, too, shall pass; and pass it does when we are easy with it.

When we feel good about ourselves, about our lives, and what we do, everything else falls into place with ease. In the right environment, everything will work itself out and require little to no effort.

We see through the eyes of god, as they say. We understand on a deeper level and are easier with others. We see unity, synchronicity, ease, and play. There is joy, cooperation, fun, love, and enlightenment. We know everything is okay.

Our best chance of being a great friend, spouse, parent, artist, citizen, or anything else, is to get aligned. We will then line up with opportunity after opportunity for what we truly desire. We will feel more peaceful and easy-going. Our lives will feel like magic. We'll have a thought about something, and then within a few minutes or hours, it'll show up. Synchronicity will become rampant in our lives, and we will feel more connected.

The world will play with us more. Everything will feel fun. The path will feel so very easy and playful. We will feel lighter and freer. We will meet up with others who are the same way or are on the path to being the same way. As we do this, we change the world around us.

Thought Clusters:

This environment is likely to compound a certain cluster of thoughts. One thought will trigger another like it, and that will trigger the next. We can spend minutes or hours thinking these types of thoughts, which feeds the energy of the environment. We rarely ever just think one of these thoughts — that's why they're called clusters. They usually pull each other into the thought process and are never isolated.

Thought clusters in alignment can be exactly or similar to the following:

"I love my life."
"Thank you for this beautiful gift."
"I am so blessed to live it every day."
"Everything always works out for me."
"I am so happy."
"Life feels good."
"I feel at peace."
"Everything is great."
"I am honored to live my life."
"Everything is perfect."

Thoughts in alignment tend to be peaceful, loving, or joyful in nature. They don't move fast, and they're not idle. There is just the perfect amount of focus on the positive. It comes easily once we are in this environment and will continue to flow until we direct our attention elsewhere and begin judging or noticing things we don't like.

This is the environment of no resistance, and therefore, the thoughts and emotions flow freely without force or resistance. This will also affect the way we remember our past and expect for our future.

We are more likely to remember the other times we felt ease and alignment. We look at our past through the eyes of understanding and gratitude. We feel warm and blessed for our journey. It all feels perfect.

We also feel ease about our future. There is no worry or paranoia about what can happen. We understand that we are the creators of our experience, and we consciously accept that power.

What To Do:

The most effective way to stay in joy, empowerment, freedom, or love is to focus on how much of it surrounds you and is within you. You can multiply it by noticing it and appreciating it more. This would be the perfect time to "take score" as they say.

Count your blessings. Make a list of all the great things in your life. Write a letter of appreciation to the people who support and love you. What a great blessing it is to have them. Focus on the love you feel in your heart. Use your friends, family, dog, the new shoes you bought; it doesn't matter what it is, as long as it brings out the feeling of love within you.

If you can find a way to always access something that reminds you of love, you will easily stay aligned. Appreciation is the fastest way to climb up because it's the same energy as love. Regardless of the subject, if you can focus on what you love or appreciate about it and talk about only that, you can shift yourself within minutes.

Share the aspects you love about it. List the parts that thrill you. Get your passion moving on the things you love. Start building positive momentum in all areas of your life by paying attention to the good. Feel blessed. Rant about it!

The Energy of Emotions

We are so quick to rant about things we hate and how much someone upset us. How often do we rant about how great life is? How many people rant about their wonderful spouses? You're more likely to hear rants about all the things they don't do than about all the things they do. Focus on the good things, and you will multiply them.

You can start from a general and wide place and then narrow it in on something specific. Or you can start with something simple like having appreciation for this moment right now or the tea you're drinking, and then make it bigger and wider.

You can write it as a list, you can write it in a letter or journal, you can write it in any way that feels good. Let's do a short rant now as an example. I'm going to do one that's easy for me because I already feel good about it. I'll keep it more general and less personal so it's easier to follow along.

"I love that this book exists. I love that there is so much knowledge in the world and that people are so open to teaching others what they know. I love that hundreds of thousands of people went in search of knowledge and wisdom before me just so I could live in a world full of so much advancement and technology.

I love that I come from a long line of truth seekers who have risked their lives and reputations just to have a better understanding of life. I love the philosophers, teachers, and great minds that helped advance society.

I love the inventors of the world. What a blessing it is to have all these great minds who come up with gadgets and machinery that make our lives easier.

I love that I am on the farthest technological edge that humanity has ever been on. I love that I can just look up everything I've ever been curious about on a little screen that fits into my pocket. I love that I have access to a world of information about anything I want. I love that I could study anything I want and become an expert on anything that grabs my interest.

I love that I can just open a screen and have access to anyone anywhere in the world. I love that people are becoming more connected through technology. I love that children are born having mastery in technology and fifteen-year-old geniuses are already solving medical mysteries and finding cures for diseases.

I love reading about the smart and talented youth who are changing the world through the evolution of their consciousness. I love that I get to be here right now to witness the revolutionary growth they are inspiring.

I love that no matter what happens, human beings always find a way. I love how resourceful and brave we are. I love that we have such great examples of human courage and bravery. I love how inspiring my fellow human beings are.

I love that even after disasters, human beings come together. I love that we lift together and pull together and build together. I love that we have an innate goodness within us that always comes out when things look dark. I love that we can inspire and uplift each other no matter what. I love being a part of this global community of uplifters and teachers.

I love that I can sit down with anyone and have a conversation about what they believe. I love that this world is more connected now than it ever has been before. It gives me great hope that we're all headed in the right direction, and that feels good."

Did you feel that energetic upliftment? I did. But then again, it was my rant. I focused on the parts that made me feel good and don't bring up any resistance.

Do that with any of your own subjects, and you'll feel better about it every time you return to it. You'll feel better about the world you live in and the people who surround you. You'll feel more joy and freedom in your life. You'll feel more connected.

You can do general rants like I did with technology and knowledge or you can do specific rants about your family, career, kids, or house. Whatever you have, you can find something to love about it. It's just a matter of focus.

I could have chosen to focus on the opposite side of that topic and mentioned all of the things that are not good with technology and humanity. I could have brought the focus on murderers or wars or diseases. But what would that have solved? It would have left both of us in a more negative state, and that doesn't help you or me. It doesn't help the world. We are better for the world when we feel better. Our pain and anger don't help anyone—not us, not others.

When writing or speaking a rant, stay away from topics that bring up resistance. If you write a positive line but don't really believe it, you're feeding the opposite. You're shifting your energy back down. It's not about the words; it's about the feeling. Choose the words that perpetuate the feeling you want. Don't pick words that sound pretty or nice in theory. "I believe we all can live in peace." Sounds beautiful in theory, but do you really believe it? If not, then don't focus on peace. Focus on the topics that don't make you feel like a liar or like you're faking it.

It must FEEL real. "I feel more peaceful in my life." "I have hope that we can have more peace." Soften it by using words like process or hope. "I am in the process of obtaining more peace." That sounds much better than "I am peaceful."

Find softer versions of words and sentences, and you can rant about anything in your life. If you are general enough, you can rant about every topic. You can magnify the good and free-flowing energy within you, and it will spill over into your life and experiences.

You're welcome to rewrite the one I wrote or write your own. Just keep your focus on what's working. Think about what you love. You can make lists if you like, or you can do it like I did and just write about it in a journal. You can also create a positivity rant journal where you rant about all of the things you love.

Some days, it may not be easy; in which case, just find ease where you can. Take a ten-minute walk and appreciate the flowers on the way. Notice the freedom of the birds. Change your scenery to change your mood.

But if you are in alignment, if you feel really good, if you feel on top of the world, then rant. It doesn't have to be to others. Rant to yourself or rant on paper. All of that will be much easier and more natural to do once you're here. All you have to do is keep it going by focusing on it more. The energy will feed itself—let it.

If you have to force it, then you're doing the opposite and introducing resistance. Find ease where you can—for five minutes, ten minutes—and then shift your focus on the things you love. Keep your focus there as long as you can until you feel your heart expanding. When your chest feels expansive, you're there. Or better yet, here.

You are now aligned.

The Energy in Emotions

There are many other emotions that were not listed in the previous environments. You're welcome to pick the environment that is closest to that emotion. Most of them are lesser or greater degrees of each other. For example, embarrassed is a lesser degree of shame. Calm is a lesser degree of peace. You can use your best judgment to sort the other emotions accordingly.

The most important thing to learn about emotions, regardless of the emotion, is how to find your own ease and relief from them. Most resistance is perpetuated by the denial or disallowance of emotion. So your main goal should be relief because relief releases resistance and allows the energy to flow faster.

When the energy is slow moving, our thoughts and emotions feel heavier. They add more weight to how we feel in our bodies. The thought "I can't do this." will not make you get up out of bed faster, walk faster, drive faster, or arrive there earlier. It will physically slow you down.

You can always tell how fast or slow the energy is flowing by how you feel. Your emotions will indicate energy flow, so it's important to become more conscious of how you feel.

Children who weren't taught how to manage their feelings become adults who don't know how to manage their feelings. This sets us up to become default creators who repeat the same experiences through different people. We become reactionaries who settle for our lives.

We can establish a lot of momentum in our childhoods with certain emotional environments, making it easier for us to return to them as adults. The more we practice, the more momentum we build. It becomes easier and easier to become depressed or angry. We can be triggered by a few words from others.

If we grow up in a parental environment of fear or anger, it can set one or more of these environments as our default dipping position when we have an emotional drop later in life. We internalize the way we are treated as children, and that sets our beliefs and expectations as adults.

We can change our default or home environments by moving ourselves up more regularly. It's true, we didn't have control over the way we were raised and treated as children, but we have control over our emotions now. We don't have to have the same emotional environments in which we grew up. They just become automatic comfort zones for us. What we are used to begins to feel familiar and safe even if we don't like it; even if we hate it.

You might not be able to "control" your emotions in the sense that you get to choose what you feel, but you can manage them. You can choose how to express it, how to ease it, how to move it into a better feeling. If you practice that enough, you can build faster pathways to better feelings. Next time someone lies to you, instead of raging you might feel more inclined to calmly talked to them about their choices. Becoming the victim of a lie or betrayal might lead you to a place of wanting to understand instead of wanting to punish. That would be considered emotional growth.

You have default responses and ways to deal with each emotion. You've been practicing it your whole life. Now you get to choose what you want to practice and how you want to practice it. You get to choose what you strengthen.

It's the same with how we direct our energy. If withdrawing our energy into ourselves is our comfort and makes us feel more in control of our lives, then that is what we will always do when we feel uncertain or insecure. If pushing our energy out on others makes us feel safer and more in control, then that is what we will do when we feel threatened. However, none of these pathways and means of expression are permanent. They're just learned behavior. Usually we learned it from an early age.

We can jump from environment to environment, energy expression to energy expression, throughout the day. We can experience a wide range of emotions and expression that will differ from person to person. We can become anxious and withdraw our energy with one person and then feel fun and free flowing with another. It mostly depends on our expectation and momentum.

We establish emotional environments with people, places, and things. We can physically move away from our home and establish other emotional environments elsewhere, but every time we return home, we will automatically drop or rise to our family/home environment. This is more about emotional environments than physical environments.

We can be easily angered with one person or always feel joy around another, regardless of where we are standing physically. The more we get angry around someone, the more we expect to get angry around them the next time. We begin to build momentum with each interaction. Then, we don't expect anything more than what we've established.

Our expressions of emotion and energy don't change because they've become habits. We habitually expect and respond to others, and they do the same in return. However, we can break that cycle through our conscious choices. We can break that cycle through how we direct our energy.

Energy is the creative force of the universe; if we direct it onto something, we infuse that thing with life. It is the life force. It IS life. We get to choose what we give life to with our focus and attention. We get to choose where we direct our energy. Do we want to give more life to combative relationships and angry interactions? Do we want to feed more of what we don't want? Just because we've been choosing that as a default habitual response doesn't mean we have to keep doing it.

Our default emotional environment has the most life because we've directed a lot of energy into it over the years and decades. It has a lot of energetic momentum, so it's easier to dip into. It feels more comfortable to be there because it's familiar. We might not want to be there anymore, but it's become an emotional habit and home, so we return to it frequently.

The more we practice certain emotions, the more momentum we build within them. As the momentum builds, it creates emotional homes. The good news is we can change it through practice. We can change it by creating new habits. We can change it by shifting and building more momentum in other environments. All it takes is practice.

The Expression of Energy:

There are different speeds of flowing energy that can feel pulled in, pushed out, and free flowing. In other words, it can be described as withdrawn, forced, or present.

The first and second environments are pulled in, or withdrawn energies. They are pulled in to the self and it makes us self-conscious. Most of the time when we have withdrawn energy, we feel left out. We feel like we don't really exist in a room. We can easily disappear in a crowd. Since we keep our energies pulled in, other people can't really feel our presence.

We tend to be victimized and targets of pushed-out or forced energy. We can become very sensitive to everyone else's energy around us and often feel bothered by others. Energy is slow moving and is mostly expressed internally, toward the self.

We often don't speak up for ourselves and will trigger illness in our bodies just to get out of doing things we can't say no to. Withdrawn energy is a harbinger of illness. The illness will provide an excuse, a sense of comfort that we don't have to do anything we don't want to do. The illness provides the buffer we need between ourselves and other people. It's a form of subconscious self-wounding that occurs as a form of protection.

The energetic withdrawal is often accompanied by a physical withdrawal. We feel uncomfortable around others and dread social situations. We tend to lack boundaries and don't know how to say no. We become people pleasers who want others around us to be happy because our energy depends on their energy. If they are angry, we are miserable. If they are happy, we feel less anxious.

We also don't like being forced or pressured into anything, which is why we might manifest a migraine, fever, a random stomach illness, or a fall simply to offer us the *no* we don't have the courage to say.

We especially don't like people with pushed-out energy expression. Aggression, anger, skepticism, and pessimism (Environments 3 through 6) are all pushed-out energy expression. It mostly focuses on everything but the self. This energy either judges, blames, or fights against the outside world.

When we have pushed-out energy expression, we are loud and forceful with our beliefs and opinions. We tend to take up more space than usual and don't mind violating other people's spaces. Others can very easily feel overpowered in our presence. For us, it's about control, and we try to take control by pushing out our energy on to others.

Other people are less likely to be themselves in the presence of this energy expression. They won't be open or even honest because they might fear unwanted criticism or attack from us. Because most people withdraw in the presence of someone with pushed-out energy, we can often feel as though we are in control. Others will pretend to agree with us or listen to us just to avoid unpleasant altercations, and we will mistake that behavior to mean that we are in control, are respected, or were heard in that situation. When in reality, others just don't want to be around the energy expression for very long, so they'll say or do what they can to minimize the energetic push.

It's not pleasant being around us when we push our energy on others, and most people try to avoid it because it can be draining for them.

Environments 8 through 10 are all free-flowing energy expressions. When we are present and in the moment, we tend to have free-flowing energy, an equal amount of in and out. Nothing is forced out, and nothing is held back. It is energy in balance.

Through enough practice, we can rise faster through the environments. We can become very present in depression and then find ourselves immediately in hope. We can breathe through our anger and then find ourselves in peace.

Sitting meditation is the best form of becoming present and allowing the energy to balance itself. Through meditation, we allow thoughts to pass without adding emotion to them. We stop the anger, the frustration, the insecurity, and we allow ourselves to be in the moment. The energy balances, and we feel better.

Whether it's walking meditation, sitting meditation, or working on our art. Any activity that brings our focus front and center without force or fear is a free-flowing energy activity.

All of the activities that are mentioned at the end of each environment are designed to bring us into the present moment within that environment. They are designed as ease activities to move us up little by little. You are welcome to skip most of them and just meditate. That's the best activity of them all.

We can also meditate by drawing a picture, we can meditate by writing a book, we can meditate by playing sports, or playing an instrument. All of these activities are "in the flow." They draw our attention and energy off of ourselves and off of the world around us so that all we can see, feel, or do is what is right in front of us.

The present moment is where all the power is—it's not in forcing ourselves onto others, it's not in pretending we don't exist—it's right here, right now, in the center of our miraculous body and being. Our energy is so powerful that it can create our world.

Present energy is an equal balance of give and take. It is present and aware in the moment. There is no need to pull energy back out of insecurity or push it out over fear. It's aligned and inspired by positive emotion.

We get to decide how we want to use that energy. We get to choose where we direct it. No emotional environment is bad; one simply feels better than another. It's not about wrong or right; it's about the natural process that is always leading us to peace, love, freedom, and joy, if we allow it. It is always leading us to the present moment where energy is free flowing and bountiful.

Stuck Energy:

There is no stuck energy. It is always moving through us, even if it's a slow movement. Even when it feels like we are filled up with a lot of bad feelings. Even when we withdraw it, it's still flowing—just slowly. Energy is like a moving river: full but flowing.

Let's imagine we feel stuck in frustration, and every time we think of a particular situation, we feel frustrated. We just can't see a way out. It feels unmoving. Stuck.

Even though we might stay in that emotional environment for a longer period of time, it doesn't mean that the energy is stuck. The energy is always new and refreshing. In every moment, the energy wants to move up naturally. It's like the course of the river, naturally moving in one direction.

However, we keep looking at the frustrating situations and reenergizing the frustrating environment. It's not so much stuck as it is renewed in the *same way* each time we look at it. The feeling is flowing, even if the feeling is "stuckness."

We keep feeding the same situation with frustration and think it's become stuck. But energy can't get stuck in emotions; it must flow even if it's flowing more of the same. "Stuckness" is an emotion itself, not a behavior. We FEEL stuck, we are not stuck. It is a degree of feeling frustrated.

So you can feel a lot of frustration but the emotion can't get stuck. You can find ways to ease it, calm it, relieve it, and move it. Once you do that, you will begin to see answers and solutions you couldn't see from the frustrated stuck environment. There are no answers there, only more frustration. That's why it feels stuck.

This is why meditation is so powerful. It interrupts the thoughts that keep reenergizing the same feelings. It calms the mind, which calms the emotions, which calms the energy. If we don't loop it back, it will naturally take us to a better-feeling place. The reason why taking a walk or distracting ourselves feels better is because energy is naturally moving in a free-flowing stream if we just stop bringing resistance and struggle into it through our practiced thoughts and reactions.

Every time we look at a problem or issue, it naturally wants to move forward. By paying attention to it, we activate its movement. But so often, we don't let it move. We add more shame to it. We add more rage to it. We keep ourselves in these environments because we judge our process. We've been conditioned to see certain emotions and behaviors as negative and something we should be ashamed of. We become frustrated with a natural process that everyone goes through. We hate ourselves for being human, and then we feel stuck.

It's important to allow people to have their processes as well. Some people can jump from anger to hope because they have more momentum going in hope and can easily get back there. Some people need to move up one by one. Others might spend more time in aggression because they've spent a lot of time feeling powerless.

It's important to allow the natural process to occur without making ourselves or others wrong. If we judge all aggressors, we deny the aggression within us. When we deny that, we are capable of doing similar things, and that keeps us in the environment of aggression. Raging against a raging man is still raging. We are not "better" aggressors; we just justify our actions better than other people's actions. But so do they.

An act of aggression is an act of aggression, and if we remove ourselves from the possibility of being in that environment, we slow down our natural process. Not only is everyone capable of becoming aggressors, but also we have all been many times. It's about healthy aggression. It's about healthy expression. It's about a healthy process that doesn't harm others. Resisting aggression in general can keep us in a cycle of recreating it. It must be accepted and released. To be human is to feel aggression. To be human is to feel sadness. You cannot deny your humanity and expect to feel good about yourself.

Energy wants to move naturally and not be forced or pushed out. If we're in doubt, we can't force ourselves into hope. We have to let it happen or else we'll feel stuck. Anytime we try to force an emotion or outcome, we begin to feel frustrated and stuck. It's our resistance against allowing emotions to happen and finish their process that creates more suffering, cycles, and the feeling of "stuckness." Let it pass, let it go, and let it flow.

Forceful Energy:

Forceful "pushed-out" energy expression comes from two places: insecurity from fear (Environment 2) or aggression from fear (Environment 3). Most of the lower environments are based in the general emotion of fear. Whether we withdraw from the world, feel anxious about it, rage against it, or blame it, we are in a state of fear.

Anger and rage are attempts at hiding fear and vulnerability. They can give us a false feeling of power over our lives when we are feeling fear deep down inside. They can make us push out our energy onto others just to hide the fact that we feel disempowered or out of control.

Many people who become angry also become out of control because the dominant feeling underneath anger is a fear of being out of control. We can't force our energy onto something to manipulate it into our desired outcome or behavior. We can't force energetic matches. We can only guide our energy to flow in a particular direction through our focus. And whether or not something responds depends on its own energy.

Forcing energy is a fear-based attempt and will only attract a response that is also fear based. Situations, events, and circumstances work through matches in energy, which is an easy process. It's easy for an angry person to match up with something that continues to feed their anger. It's easy for a passionate person to match up with something that carries the momentum of their passion. It's easy to continue to feel anxious; it's easy to continue to feel frustrated. Energy feeds itself through momentum and there's plenty of it in each environment.

Manipulation, control, and force create different possibilities and avenues. Doing the same thing through ease, versus using force, will bring us very different results. All of the effort we use to control or manipulate will just keep us struggling and will eventually exhaust us. It is energetically draining.

Letting go is a form of energetic surrender. It is a type of release that frees us of the resistance that is blocking natural flow. All of that heaviness is finally eased, so it allows for better circumstances to come into our experience. It opens a pathway that was previously closed through force. By letting go of effort and force, we are finally allowing natural solutions to appear. By letting go of control, we open up opportunities for what we desire.

We don't have to struggle or apply effort or work hard to "make" something happen. We simply allow it to happen by nurturing the emotional environment first. This allows the possibilities to reveal themselves to us. We allow the avenues to open up instead of trying to force them open. Allowing is not struggling, not fighting, not forcing.

Allowing doesn't mean that we don't "do" anything. We do, we just do it from a positively inspired environment. Our actions are coming from a place of ease or passion or joy, so they return more possibilities and avenues for those things. It feels faster and easier, and it doesn't require a lot of "work." When we are in the right environment, it's not work. It's fun, it's play, it's enjoyable social interactions. It's creating and building and loving the process. It's 13-hour days that don't feel like a grind. If you're in the right environment, it never feels like work.

If you're in a lower environment, everything will feel like work. Getting out of bed will feel like a struggle. Even thinking thoughts will feel hard. These environments will not offer the pathways to joy, not unless you've practiced them.

An action from an aggressive environment will rarely bring us an opportunity for joy or peace. It might bring us a bit of relief, but whatever action we commit from there will have a consequence that we will then have to deal with, thus prolonging the peaceful or joyful outcome.

It's better to find the relief and ease first, move up to a better environment, and then act. If we can tap into our passion, we won't need to work "hard" ever again. Other people will see it as working hard, and we will see it as fun and ease.

Energetic Matches:

Everything is an energetic match. You and your car, your house, your bank account, your spouse, your children, and your job are all matches to your energy. They are reflecting back your movement and expression of energy.

This does not mean that you have "bad" energy if you aren't married, don't have enough money, or don't own property. Maybe you don't want any of those things. Perhaps those things hold a different level of value to you.

Either way, most of what we create today is a reflection of an old energy pattern that we keep alive through beliefs. It was something we were taught as children that we internalized and now expect.

A lot of us were taught unworthiness. Whether it was society, family, friends, teachers, classmates, or our culture. We were taught we are not good enough, not smart enough, not pretty enough, not funny enough, not man enough, not something enough. We were taught that something was missing within us and we had to work for the rest of our lives to get it. Then, we would be complete and worthy.

Wherever you are standing right now, you can create a better life. Believe that and your emotions will begin to shift immediately. You will know you are creating a better life through the small synchronicities that come your way as energetic matches. You will begin to meet the right people; you will discover the right books, the right seminars, and the right opportunities.

You will feel a powerful resonance to words, to signs, or people. It'll feel like the universe is speaking to you. It is. Energy matches energy, and when you begin to flow freely you'll match up with others on that same level.

When two free-flowing people meet, a type of resonance happens within them that can feel powerful. This can feel like soul mates or an instant lifelong best friend that you've just met. It can't be denied either way. You'll feel it in your core.

The most powerful thing you can do after learning methods to ease yourself is to work on your self-worth. When that rises, so will the quality of your life. You will look at everything around you differently.

You won't think of "no" as a rejection. You'll see it as a form of protection. You'll see it as a wrong match for you and you'll let it go with ease. You'll move onto better opportunities. However, with low self-worth we think that a no means we are not worthy of it, but really a no means it's not a match to our energy. It's not a match to who we are and what we desire. Not because we're not good enough for it, but because it's not on our level. There is something better, something more fitting for us.

The more we stay in a free-flowing energy state, the easier it is for us to return to it. The easier it is for us to create from it. The easier it is for us to trust it. It will soon become a dominant energy within us, and we will begin to pull in matching experiences.

Your "work" in every situation is always your own energy. It's not about forcing someone else's actions, or changing someone else's mind. You can't force a non-matching person to become a match to you. By using force or control, you'll dip down into the aggressive environment. Then, you'll pull in matches from there.

It's not about what someone else said or did. It's always about where you are with your energy. As Deepak Chopra said, "What other people think of you is none of your business." What matters is what you think of you. Once you feel better about yourself, you'll match up with others who feel the same way. They'll reflect back your level of self-esteem and self-love.

It's your own power of belief that has any affect on your life and experiences. Work on yourself, and everything in your life will improve. Your relationships, your job opportunities, your circle of friends, your health. Everything will rise with your energy.

Read the books, go to the seminars, go to therapy, exercise, take time for yourself, eat right, get creative, find processes of relief and ease. Take care of yourself, and you can move your default environment into hope, enthusiasm, content, or joy.

No one is ever stuck in an environment. Every moment, there is an option for a better-feeling thought or a better-feeling action. If we just follow our emotional instincts, they will lead us to the actions that bring us more peace, healing, and joy.

Soon enough, we won't need to do exercises or processes because the way we live our lives will be our everyday exercise. Finding ease in the moment will become easier. We'll find that we want to take more walks or draw more. Soon, we'll start feeling better about our whole lives. We'll take more trips to the beach, or we'll take up meditation. We won't do anything to purposely move ourselves up; we'll just find that we're automatically doing what makes us feel better. Then, we will become matches to the things that keep us feeling better and better.

The Ease of Thoughts:

All matter is energy. Your body, the table, the bicycle, the computer, this book, and all other forms of matter are pulsating with energy. If we want to pull something into our experience, we have to match it with our energy. Most matches are easy because they're matches to our dominant thoughts and feelings. To change the matches, we must change our thoughts and feelings.

Opportunities will then open for us to reach our desires. Some opportunities will be obvious, and others will be subtle. Some will take just few steps; others will take more. Either way, it won't be a difficult path. If it's difficult, it's not a complete match. Some part of it is being forced. Maybe there's an aspect of it you don't believe you can have. Maybe it clashes with your sense of worthiness or purpose.

Thoughts are easy to think. However, one thought might feel one way, and another thought might feel another way. Some things are easier to attract than others because we have prejudgments that add resistance and slow down attraction.

There are no hard thoughts to think, only thoughts with resistance. You can sit right now and imagine yourself as a wealthy entrepreneur who travels the world and meets a lot of people. The thinking is easy. But how do you feel about it? Does it feel possible? Does it feel likely? Do you believe it? Does it bring up anxiety? Or fear? Maybe feelings of unworthiness? Lack of opportunities?

Did it bring up additional thoughts like, "Yeah, right; how would I afford that?" "That would never happen." "I will never be wealthy." The emotions and level of belief about the initial thought will bring up more thoughts that will either create resistance or ease it. If you don't believe, it will feel "hard" because some aspect is not a match yet.

On the other hand, we might attract it as a negative experience. We can attract a free vacation that turns out to be a nightmare. We can attract a luxury car that always breaks down. We can attract a rich spouse who cheats on us and makes us cry every night. It's not the vacation, car, or spouse in itself that determines whether something is a good attraction or a bad one—it's how it makes us feel.

When we feel disbelief about something, it compounds the thoughts with similar thoughts that continue the feeling of disbelief. It's not so much about the thinking—because we all can think about everything in existence—it's also about the feeling behind the thought. What does it bring up? Anxiety? Disbelief? Anger? Jealousy? That will show you where your energy is on that subject and therefore what you're a match to. It's not just positive thinking; it's also positive feeling and believing. We can think positively and not believe anything we're thinking. We call that wishful thinking because it lacks belief. And the only reason it lacks belief is because of our personal value systems. We judge the things around us as big and small, expensive or cheap, but there are no big or small thoughts, there are no cheap emotions. There is just energy matching up with similar energy. It can match up just as easily with an island as it can with a penny.

The speed and ease through which it comes will depend on the thinker of the thought. Do you believe you need to work hard and struggle to create wealth? Do you believe it can be done through enjoying your work? Do you believe it can be done through having fun with your passion projects? If you believed and you were dominantly in the passion environment, it would be an easy manifestation for you. The energy would flow, the opportunities would come, and you would take them.

If you were in a lower environment, you might not see the opportunities, you might not believe the opportunities, or you might even block them altogether. What you believe has a stronger impact on what comes than where you're standing. You can get to your desired destination. There is a path to it from where you are now. Believe it. Let your thoughts come easily about what you want. Allow it to sit in you without resistance.

Questions and Answers:
Our minds are designed to find answers. If we pose a question, our minds will automatically search our realms of possibility to find answers. The questions we ask ourselves on a daily basis play an important role in our emotional wellness.

For instance, if we asked ourselves, "Why is my life so hard?" Our minds would automatically search for the answers. If we asked, "Why can't I get it right?" Again, our minds would come up with a list of reasons.

What if we changed the questions we asked? What if we asked, "What would make me feel better right now?" "What would I rather do right now?" "What would bring me ease in this moment?" "What can I do to find more relief?" "What would make me happy in this moment?" "Whom could I call who would help me feel better?" "Would a walk help?" "If I distracted myself, would that bring me ease?" "What can I do?"

If we change the type of questions we ask ourselves, we can change our emotions in the moment. When we ask negatively focused questions, it leads our minds to negative answers that leave us feeling disempowered. We can shift our mood onto something better feeling and something more productive by asking positively focused questions.

Usually, in the lower environments, we get a different set of questions that perpetuate those types of feelings. But we can also write better questions down and place them somewhere noticeable like on a board or on a dresser. It would greatly help ease our emotional states if we were to practice asking ourselves better questions.

When an event occurs that feels unwanted, we must ask ourselves a few questions to understand the match. The first question is, "How does this make me feel?" It might not be the obvious answer. If we've been betrayed and we feel angry, anger might be the second emotion to feeling vulnerable or targeted first, which is more indicative of Environment 2 than 4.

The second question is, "Where else do I currently feel this way?" If the event makes us feel powerless and not in control of our lives, then we might realize that at work we also feel powerless and not in control. It might seem like different events that are completely separate from each other, but it's the same feeling, which means it's a match. It was a dominant emotion because we practiced it every day at work. Energy compounds itself and repeats through similar feeling experiences, which will feed our dominant feeling. If we can't find a way to heal, work on, or ease the initial feeling, it will keep pulling in similar matches.

Questions will not only help us see where we are emotionally, but they will also help move us up. If we ask the right questions, they can greatly benefit us. Our response will show us the truth of how we feel.

We can't fake an emotion. We can fake the appearance of an emotion to another human being, but we can't fake the energy within us. For that reason, we can't force or manipulate experiences. They come as a response to the energy we have, not to the energy we want to have.

For instance, visualizations don't work if every time we look at a beautiful house we feel as if we can never have it. Affirmations will work against us if we say we love ourselves and then feel unworthy saying it. If we don't really believe it, there is no point in doing the process. The point of the process is the feeling it creates, not the words we use.

When we force a process just to get the outcome, it works against us. We will feed the opposite of what we want. Looking at something we don't have and trying to pretend we do have it only feeds the energy of the lack. We will continue not having it. The feeling reciprocates similar energies. So if the feeling is false, it won't work. Or if the feeling is a lack of something, then that is what we will attract: the lack of that thing.

Everything we want is because we want the feeling we'll get when we have it. The easiest way to have it is to feel how we would feel if we had it now.

We can find the emotion from the things we don't have by focusing on the things we do have that bring forth the same emotions. This will feed the energy and bring in more. It might not look like what we think it will look like. It might come in another form, but the feeling behind it will be a match.

If we want love or freedom, then we have to practice those emotions in other areas of our lives. This will attract more love or freedom into our lives. As the Buddha said, "We get there when we believe we are already there." If we feel the feeling behind what we want, it will bring it into our experience in one form or another.

First, we must be completely honest with ourselves. What do we really want? Which emotions do we value above others? When we do find what the emotion is, we have to practice it daily and see it around us. Where else do we feel secure? What else brings us pleasure? Where do we have love now? It could be our dog or our friends or something else. It doesn't have to be huge or wild. It could be simple but still have the same feeling.

Every emotion we want, we already have access to. If we want to add to the degrees, all we have to do is focus on the amount we do have, which feeds it our energy. As we feel it more and more, we can see it grow in our lives.

Speeding Up The Process:
The most powerful process is the one of appreciation. It's a fast and easy multiplier of free-flowing energy. When

we focus on the things we feel appreciation for, they multiply in our lives.

If you can incorporate a gratitude journal into your daily processes, you'll change your default environment in just a few days.

There are two processes that yield fast results: one is meditation, and the other is a gratitude journal. One will stop negative emotion; the other will accelerate positive emotion. You can use them back-to-back. Meditate for ten minutes and then write five things you feel grateful for in a gratitude journal.

It's best to do these processes at the end of your day. You will clear your mind and energy with meditation, and this will help you sleep better. Then, reflect on five things you feel grateful for. It could be the delicious ice cream you ate, the beautiful blue flower you saw on your walk, a compliment from a co-worker, etc. This will help you appreciate the day that has passed, and it will set up more good experiences for the following day. As you begin to notice more things you appreciate on a daily basis, your days will get better and better.

It's important to find a process that works for you. Not all processes work for everyone. Feel free to adjust or change any of the processes I've mentioned in the previous environments. The goal is ease, relief, and to feel better. What you do isn't as important as how you feel when you're doing it. You might even grow tired of some processes and find that they don't work anymore. That's okay. Find another one that brings you the same feeling.

Some people use positive affirmations, and they feel good, while others might feel doubtful or skeptical when saying them. It's not what you say — it's how you feel saying it. If it makes you angry or brings up more resistance, then switch up something. Change a process. Do it your way. This is about your ease; it's about your feelings.

They are emotional environments, not mental environments. The energy will line up with the emotions, not the words. For example, if you're saying, "I love him," but you're feeling anxiety as you say it because you don't really trust him, then you're not in Environment 10 where the love is—you're in Environment 2, where the anxiety and insecurity is. The feeling of anxiety will direct the energy of the relationship, not the "loving" words. The feeling will direct the energy every time, so you can't lie or pretend your way there.

The energy doesn't hear what we say; energy only understands energy. However, we can use our words to bring forth the emotions we want. If we can change the way we tell a story from our past to make ourselves feel better, we will shift that story and the energy associated with it.

Even saying something like, "I was really angry, but now I'm learning to be easier about it," will still work because it's true. It won't create resistance within you, and it feels softer. "Sometimes, I still get angry about it, but I'm willing to find ease with it." Speak true statements so you don't trigger more resistance, but be soft about the way you tell it. Always leave a story in a hopeful place.

Moving up the emotional levels can take years, months, weeks, days, or hours, depending on whether we allow the natural movement through them or whether we cycle back and forth among two or three environments.

If we consciously allow it as it's happening, it will become easier the next time we talk about it. As the momentum of ease builds, we can work through something in a matter of hours or minutes. We might soon discover that we dip into hope as a default emotional reaction instead of depression, anxiety, or rage.

Different topics linger in different environments because we leave them there by repeating the same stories in the same way.

Money might be in insecurity, while relationships might be in doubt. Children might be in hope, while career is in anger. We can become very joyful thinking about our children, and then become very angry thinking about their father. It all depends on how we choose to look at each event, person, and circumstance in our lives. Issues naturally want to move into better-feeling places; we are the only sources who keep them stuck in certain emotions.

The words we choose to share, the feelings we emote, make all the difference in which direction we're moving. They will also attract similar people.

With each environment, except depression and joy, there are two options: up or down. We will meet people who will offer us a chance to move up in emotions or to move down. Each conversation, encounter, meeting, or story is an opportunity to move either way. The direction we're moving in will be evident by how much relief or ease we feel. If it's getting harder, more stressful, and more upsetting, then we're moving down.

To get a clear idea of where you stand with each topic, take a sheet of paper and number each line 1 through 10. Then as you think about the subjects, write them on the line by the number that corresponds with the emotional environment. When you think about it, does it make you feel angry, hopeful, irritated?

This way, you know where to begin when doing any emotional work to move up a subject. You don't have to dip down to depression and start from there if you're only feeling disappointment about your income.

As you work through easing each subject, come back to it and do it again. After about a week or two, check to see where each subject feels. It could have moved higher or lower, depending on what was triggered through the exercises.

Just making the list might create ease. You might suddenly feel glad that you're only disappointed with your income and not depressed about it. Just feeling the relief by looking at it will move it up into hope.

If you're feeling disappointed about income, wait until you're hopeful or excited about another subject, and then work out your income. You can use the feeling of one environment to move the thoughts forward in another. If you leave them in a softer place, you can return to them there. Move them only from a better place. Don't start thinking about your disappointing income when you're depressed. You'll move it down into depression.

It is in our best interest to find as much ease as we can in all of the areas in our lives. As we do this, we will feel lighter and freer.

This doesn't mean we have to go to a spa all day or meditate for eight hours. A spa might make us frustrated, thinking about all the things that need to be done back home. Meditation might make us annoyed.

Don't do what others are doing. Find what feels good for you. If washing the dishes feels easier than avoiding them and then spending an hour thinking about how you need to wash the dishes, then wash the dishes. It's about always choosing the option that feels better in the moment. You might not want option A or B, but one of them feels better than the other. Pick that. Keep picking the one that feels better of the two.

Always ask yourself, "Does this feel better or worse?" "Do I feel better doing this or that?" "Which gives me more ease?" "Which thought feels better?" "Which choice feels better?" As you pick the one that feels better over and over again, options A and B will become more pleasing.

Start where you are with what you have. You don't have to drop everything and start from scratch. Work with what is in front of you, even if you don't want what you have. If you keep noticing what you don't want, you'll hold yourself in a perpetual state of not having because you'll keep introducing resistance into your energy. Notice the easier option.

Would you feel better ditching work but then spending the whole day worried about it? Or would you feel better if you just went and did it? Which choice feels better within you? Maybe work feels angry and it would feel better to worry than to feel angry.

I can't advise you to pick one choice over another or one process over another because only you know which option would leave you feeling better. Ask yourself, "What would make me feel better right now?"

It's also best to not judge others on their processes and choices. That would keep you on a lower environment. People are only doing what would help them move up into joy. Judgment doesn't help the judged or the judge find alignment.

We can't force people into a better-feeling place. We can't bomb people into alignment. We can't beat or punch people into making better choices. Better choices are a natural result of a better emotional environment. We have to let people naturally move up. If we can support them and help them find ease, then great! But we can't push them or condemn them into a better environment. It just doesn't work. Let people have their processes.

Processes aren't just about a paper and a pen; it's not just about meditation or relaxation. It's about making choices day in and day out. It's about picking the process that brings us the least amount of resistance. It's about being conscious of how we feel in each moment and choosing the action that feels the best.

Joy may not yet be an option in this circumstance, but doubt is a better choice than rage. Hope is a better choice than pessimism. Pick the one that brings the most ease or relief. Ask yourself which one feels better. And once you choose, don't make yourself wrong for it and dip back down. In every moment, there is another choice and another and another.

Bring yourself back up to a more positive-feeling place and let the environment inspire the actions you take. Don't call up someone and yell at them because you think it's going to make you feel better. Get to a better-feeling place, and then call them. Perhaps in the better-feeling place you don't feel inspired to call them at all—then don't. Find more ease first. Let the choices come naturally to you.

You don't ever have to talk yourself into something that feels good. When it happens, you naturally move into it. If you don't, then you're in doubt; you're somewhere else. If you have to worry about a choice, it's being made on a lower environment.

Ease and relief are choices we make every day. They are the difference between moving up or dipping down. We can train ourselves into finding the ease in each moment. We can calm our stress and anxiety choice by choice, moment by moment.

Once you practice enough of relief and ease, you'll create more momentum in positivity, and you'll be able to make better choices about all of those things that used to upset you. You'll be inspired into action from a better emotional environment, which will create a more favorable outcome for you.

You want to be in a space of positive momentum before you act, decide, or help someone else. Answers will be clearer and easier. Things will move faster. You'll feel better about all of your decisions and options.

You want to be in alignment as much as possible because from alignment, all things are possible. All things are doable. Challenge becomes opportunity.

You will focus your attention on the solutions instead of the problems. You will bring your attention to the hopeful and inspiring aspects instead of the daunting tasks of what needs to be done. You will feel inspired into action through joy, freedom, and peace; not obligated from guilt, shame, or fear.

Align your energy and watch how everything else lines up for you.

The Energy of You:

Your power is greater than you have ever realized, and once you know who you really are, you'll never settle for anything less. You'll crave the adventure, the passion, the fun. You'll seek out deep connections and meaningful relationships with everyone and everything. You'll see life around you as lively and exciting. Your curiosity will drive you into new ideas and journeys. You'll experience life the way it's meant to be lived, through love and alignment.

You'll see that this life is your playground, and other people are extensions of you. You'll feel the connection with everything in existence through your shared energetic lineage. You'll feel out every situation, and you'll learn to trust your intuition. You'll "know" more without learning. You'll see more without trying. You'll create more experiences intentionally and deliberately.

Every "thing" that exists is energy, and you will feel your powerful connection with it all. Everything around you will respond to you differently. Animals will be more receptive of you, people will be more cooperative with you, solutions will line up before you even realize you have a problem, you will feel harmony on all levels in your body and being.

Matter is simply condensed energy vibrating in a slow speed, and you are a unique manifestation of pulsating, life-affirming energy. Space gives us the illusion of separation, but energy connects us all. You are a piece of the source of all life in the universe. A raindrop in an ocean of mosaic energy.

Who you are is forever alive. Your organic matter of cells, muscles, and organs might decay, but energy can never die. It is neither created nor destroyed. It is merely transformed from one form to another. Who you are, as energy, existed before, and it will exist again and again.

You are a part of the stream of life and you can never step out of its flow. You can slow down and speed up through your emotions, but it will never stop flowing regardless of what form you take on.

This moment is perfect because this moment is the jumping-off place of your alignment. Here is where it begins, and here is all that matters now. Here is where you feel, and here is where you create. Right here, right now is the start of your new life. It is the start of new adventures and new experiences. A new world of possibilities is available to you through the elevated emotion you feel as you're reading these words.

Do you feel excited? Can you sense something shifting, opening, flowing within you right now? Can you feel the difference in your body, in your emotions, in your thoughts? Can you feel the power of possibility? Can you feel that the whole world is lining up and synching up with you right now?

You are the true essence of the energy you feel right now. You are the extension of source energy, the extension of life force, the extension of the power that creates worlds. Can you feel that right now? That's the energy of you.

Welcome to the God space.

"If you want to find the secrets of the universe, think in terms of energy, frequency, and vibration."
–Nikola Tesla, Physicist and Inventor.

CPSIA information can be obtained
at www.ICGtesting.com
Printed in the USA
FSHW02n2312280518
48750FS

9 781500 203917